DEAR DISH RAG READERS,

IT'S HERE!

You are holding Issue 0, the inaugural entry to the Dish Rag series. This publication is intended to be a bi-annual investigation of cultural fermentation through the lens of a new theme each issue. Cultural fermentation refers to moments of agitation and excitement that begin to form trends within our day-to-day lives. This magazine, therefore, advances a principled ambition: to draw on fermentation as both a theory and a practice as we journey across sub/human conditions and document scenes of in/animacy. The fermentation process we leverage is certainly not to preserve culture. Its aim, in an alchemical style, is to create something new and unfamiliar—even unpredictable.

Our inaugural issue opens with caves. The cave has long functioned as a site of mysterious importance for civilizations spanning thousands of years. As such, the cave exists as an important indicator of the cultural volume that lives in the depths of the Earth, buried under layers of time. In this issue, we use this subterranean space to explore some pretty expansive topics: cheese cave etymology, the urban rehoming of swiftlets, the history of Renaissance gardens and grottos, the end of an era at a club known as "the rave cave," pseudoscientific medications, and the astrological symbolism of the cave, amongst others.

The cave is a physical site from which archaeologists can excavate relics of the past that reveal new histories to us. As a consequence, we must adjust our socially constructed genealogies to correspond to those, at times, destabilizing scientific discoveries. This is what creates cultural fermentation. We view the cave as a primordial scene of both the making and unmaking of worlds—where we go when our bodies or psyches are in danger, and where we leave when the boundedness of scientific discovery grows dogmatic.

We can't help but feel a certain eeriness that the Thai cave rescue mission was timed with the release of this first issue. The soccer team was only found as a result of an accident, they arguably only survived because their coach happened to be a monk with expertise in meditative practices (naturally), a fair amount of them didn't know how to swim, they almost had to stay down there for four months until monsoon season ended, a Thai Navy SEAL tragically perished in his heroic attempt to deliver supplies to the kids, and who could forget Daddy Musk showing up with a child-sized submarine he tested in a Los Angeles pool, only to call one of the divers a pedophile when he expressed that the technology was too cumbersome for use in their rescue mission. You literally can't make this stuff up. These are the kinds of stories—the ones that make you double-take when you're scrolling through your news feed—that fuel the creative spirit of High St(e)aks Media and its publication, Dish Rag Magazine (which you are now holding in your hands).

We have chosen to print this magazine instead of simply making it available as a .pdf because these are stories that should be held and consumed. And we don't want that tangible, material connection to end there. We want this to turn into a community, a platform for our friends and family to help bring more attention to whatever their creative pursuits may be. And so, without further ado, please enjoy the first iteration of our magazine. You should probably save this copy because one day it'll be worth a lot of bitcoin (allegedly).

XOXO, THE EDITORS OF DISH RAG MAG

Illustration by Cassie Tucker

issue 0 | fall 2018 | the caves issue

DISH RAG

Editor-in-Chief
Jessica Merliss

Managing Editor
Josh Aleksanyan

Online Editor
Daniel Spielberger

Art Editor
Semantha Norris

Art Direction & Design
May Parsey

Illustrator
Cassie Tucker

Photographer
Charlie Hawks

Special thanks to:
Samuel Anderson, Jennifer Schwartz,
Sam Taffel and Peter Falls

Contributors:
Jacqueline Li - jacquieli.com, @jacquieli
Brice Bischoff - bricebischoff.com, @brice_bischoff, cirrusgallery.com
Austin Irving - austinirving.com, wildingcran.com
Nicolas Baird - nicolasbaird.com
Matthias Van Dromme
Roarke Lacey - @roarkelavey
Tony Fabro and Frank Gidlewski - @kevinthedepressedcaveman
Brian Blomerth- brianblomerth.com, @pupsintrouble
Michael Koehler - mrkoehler.com, @lordofthejord

Printer
Lightning Source

Publisher
High St(e)aks Media

Distribution:
For distribution or to become
a stockist, please contact
dishragmagazine@gmail.com

Contact:
dishragmagazine@gmail.com
Twitter: @dishragmagazine
Instagram: @dishragmag
Facebook: @DishRagMag

© 2018 High St(e)aks Media.
All rights reserved. No part of this
publication may be reproduced
without written permission.

TABLE OF CONTENTS

Travis Brock Kennedy

WHAT WE DO

IN THE SHADOWS

Fig. 1 Cueva de las Manos, Santa Cruz, Argentina — Circa 13,000-9,000 BCE

SUBTERRANEAN IMAGINARIES AND SANCTIONED SPACES FOR THE ILLICIT

Caves have long captivated the human imagination. The discovery of artifacts and paintings in, for example, the Cueva de las Manos in Argentina, the Cave of Pettakere in Indonesia, Lascaux in France, the Cave of Beasts in Libya, and the Khoit Tsenkher cave in Mongolia, speak to a universal reverence for caves that is deeply innate to the human experience. By Classical Antiquity, the Greeks associated caves with the primitive, the uncanny, and, thus, the sacred. The Greek mythic tradition placed divine births, the homes of monsters, and the concealment of illicit sex in caves. As liminal spaces between the Apollonian light and order of the world above, and the Dionysian darkness and chaos of the world below, caves signified regression from the rational realm and a descent into a sacred irrationality. Caves were the domain of oracles and nymphs, visions and intoxication.

The history of the human conception of caves, writ large, is in and of itself a captivating one; but a truly fascinating aspect—and one that has gone underappreciated by the academic community—is the way fascination with caves manifested in the grottoes of Italian Renaissance gardens. The Italian villa began its life as a rural retreat for the ruling classes in antiquity. Their gardens, often sumptuous, were the pleasure playgrounds of the Caesars and their entourages. With the fall of the Roman Empire and the relentless succession of wars, power-grabs, political instability, and economic atrophy—which came to characterize Late Antiquity and the Mediaeval period—Italian villas evolved into spaces more like fortresses and barracks than the rural retreats of their imperial forebears. Their gardens, the erstwhile pleasure playgrounds of the emperors and their ephebes, were squashed by Christian moralism and turned into more restrained bits of earth relegated to the utilitarian purposes of crop cultivation.

With the Renaissance came the rebirth, at least in aesthetics, of the lost culture of classical Greece and Rome. Across Italy, the villa and its garden reclaimed their original role as seasonal retreats meant to draw the elite out of the stress of city life, and the squalor of urban space, out into an idealized version of rural splendor. The structure of the Renaissance villa, as Edith Wharton explains in *Italian Villas and Their Gardens,* is designed to draw the individual through a succession of spaces: beginning with the entrance in a formal "city" facade, one proceeds from an interior space through an informal and open "rural" facade out into gardens; first formal and architectonic, the gardens progress into ones incrementally more rustic, ending in a bosco or planned woodland that terminates imperceptibly into the actual wild space of the countryside. The point of this elaborate orchestration of space is to create an effect of enchantment that allows the individual to sense a release into nature without the loss of the comforts of civilization.

A ubiquitous feature of these gardens is the grotto—an artificial creation meant to imitate its natural counterpart in a refined way. At the Villa d'Este in Tivoli, for example, a flamboyant array of elaborately-decorated grottoes dot an even more flamboyant landscape of waterworks and foliage. True to the spirit of the era, the creators of the Renaissance garden attributed to the grottoes that they created a romanticized (even hyperbolized) version of their traditional associations in antiquity. If the caves of antiquity were the domain of the primitive, uncanny, and pagan, then the Renaissance grotto would be the sanctioned space where rigid social rules and Christian morality no longer applied. By retreating from the city to the villa, one was already moving away from the ordered to the rustic. Indeed, by retreating from the relatively formal space of the villa to the utterly informal space of the grotto, the individual was making the final descent from the Apollonian light above to the Dionysian darkness below. The grotto was the place where one gave leave of responsibility and succumbed to temptation—where lovers met and where trysts were staged, where drugs were taken,and wine was drunk with abandon.

IN A WORD, THE GROTTO WAS THE PLACE WHERE PEOPLE DID WHAT THEY DO IN THE SHADOWS,

and in so being, the Renaissance grotto offers us not merely another instance of a universal human fascination with caves, but a case study in the ways repressed societies romanticize those they perceive to be freer.

Fig. 2 Grottoes behind the Fontana dell'Ovata at the Villa d'Este, Tivoli, 1565-1570

Photograph by Jacqueline Li

 Illustration by Roarke Lacey

CONVINCING SWIFTLETS TO BONE WHERE WE WANT: URBAN CAVES AND REHOMING SWIFTLETS

Hailey Clement

Swiftlets, or cave swifts, are the only birds famous for their spit. Come mating season, pair-bonded partners excrete a mixture of protein, carbs, and iron deep in Southeast Asian caves to build sturdy nests for their babies. Echolocating their way through the darkness, they place these nests high up along the cave walls to ensure the eggs are far from predators. The nests have to be sticky enough to remain intact despite the humidity, and strong enough to fight gravity without a perch. Somehow during the Ming Dynasty,

IT WAS DECIDED THAT THESE HARD FLAPS ARE DESIRABLE AF.

Photographs by Charlie Hawks

These edible bird nests are soaked, cleaned, and then used as an ingredient in traditional Chinese medicines, or as the star of a bowl of soup. People see them as a miracle cure, claiming they help with boners, clear up the skin, fortify the immune system, clean out the digestive tract, and help with respiratory ailments, including lung cancer. Hong Kong alone imports about 100 tons annually (Mainland China follows closely behind). However, despite this much interest in the ingredient, it's surprisingly difficult to find a description of what it tastes like. Even fans of the ingredient stick to phrases like "light," "mild," and "delicate," while skeptics say it is "without a particle of taste." One descriptor is persistently cited: the soup is definitely "gloopy." Fixed to cave walls, the nests must be hard and stable enough to withstand the weight of multiple birds and their progeny. Once soaked, however, they all but dissolve into jelly-like masses.

At a high end or traditional Chinese restaurant, there's a chance that Birds Nest Soup is on the menu. One serving could quickly set you back $50. If the soup is too cheap, it is probably doctored with gussied up tapioca or something similarly slimy. These days, one gram of edible birds nest sells for a dollar fifty on the cheap this-is-so-broken-up-it-could-be-anything end. A single, whole, untreated nest can easily go for $20. That isn't even enough for one bowl of soup.

Since at least the 1400s, entrepreneurs in the Sundaic region of Southeast Asia have sought fortune in swiftlet abodes. Even Gordon Ramsay has tried his hand at swiftlet harvesting, before getting a taste of the soup, of course.

BRAVING ROACH INFESTED CAVES FILLED WITH WALL-CLIMBING SNAKES

(these roaches love them some guano, snakes adore them some swiftlet eggs), natural harvesters travel deep into the earth to find their lode. Often they scale hundreds of feet on rickety bamboo ladders, which have become permanent fixtures in the caves. After climbing to reach a handful of nests on equipment that has been degraded, under a steady stream of acidic guano, workers climb all the way down, move the ladder, then climb all the way back up again. It's not fast work. Many harvesters never actually taste the fruits of their labor—the nests are too valuable to eat. Some try their hand at climbing the walls directly to get at them faster.

IT'S NO WONDER MANY PEOPLE DIE.

Domesticating animals is humanity's go-to answer when it comes to wanting to take advantage of another species while minimizing our own species' inconvenience. Whenever we want to profit from an animal or something it produces, we seek to control it. But we just can't domesticate swiftlets. To successfully domesticate an animal, we need to be able to control its breeding (to select for desired genes), become its primary source of food (to promote dependency), and control its environment (to adapt them to our desires better). Swiftlets bond for life, determined by understudied rituals that mostly occur mid-flight, preventing us from mating the most docile or slobberiest nest builders. And they hunt for flying insect prey. Bugs don't come in bales, and even if they did, the birds wouldn't be down for those lethargic bait shop grasshoppers. When our brute force methods of trapping and compulsory matings fail, we turn to subtler means to coax animals into doing what we want. Through extensive trial and error, conveniently documented in one of the

Photographs by Charlie Hawks

many Malaysian DIY swiftlet blogs that have popped up in the past decade, would-be tycoons have figured out some ways to convince swiftlets to move

Partially due to the danger and difficulty of harvesting nests in the wild, urban cave development has boomed in Malaysia. One-time office buildings may now be husks full of near total darkness and speakers blasting "Now That's What I Call Music: Swiftlets Panic and Go |Check On Your Babies, Quick!" Driven by the allure of pie in the sky riches, aspiring swiftlet ranchers have increased in numbers by 6000%, much to the chagrin of neighbors who don't love the increase in bird shit and noise pollution.

The job doesn't end once the swiftlets flutter in to check out these swanky inner city abodes. Urban harvesters also have to convince them to move in and start a family. Rule number 1 is to make the spaces at least 4 meters by 4 meters wide. Baby swiftlets don't have a tight turning

ALL THIS FOR A GLOOPY SOUP THAT

radius, and anything smaller will have them crashing into walls.

RULE NUMBER 2 SETS THE RIGHT ATMOSPHERE.

Reducing the light intensity to 2 lux or lower, they hope to make the space cozy enough for cuddling. Some farmers are even experimenting with humidifiers to try to replicate that sweet, clammy cave air. As for food, they need to show that there's enough for the current adult swiftlets, as well as for future generations. Products like Walitein now exist to create a multi-vitamin enriched meal for the bugs that feed the swiftlet population. By mixing up some bug gruel and encouraging the local population within the chosen urban cave, farmers hope to invite swiftlets in for a feast and to assure them, subconsciously, that there is plenty more coming. With all these added amenities in formerly abandoned buildings, we're constructing better homes for these birds than for some of the people living alongside them.

GORDON RAMSAY DOESN'T EVEN LIKE.

Cro-Magnon Malibu
BY: DANIEL SPIELBERGER
PINOT

"MONICA, THESE GRAPES ARE SO RIPE, SO AMAZING."

Angelo has been eating these big purple grapes for the last ten minutes. The noon sun is hitting us, the tide is calm, and the sand is warm: we're far away from the hellhole of horse therapy and it's just the two of us, a picnic basket, and the chilled Grigio. I have been going to Malibu Creek services—aka the best horse therapy in all of southern California—for the past two months.

Each session always has a dozen other people; drug addicts, gamblers, and recent divorcees, like me, who have shelled out $500 an hour to experience the perfect breed of psychoanalysis and *My Little Pony.* My son made me do this. He signed me up the day after I crashed the Mustang during a night out on the town. He signed me up after Ricky told me he was moving to Boston for the indefinite future. Yes, I am spewing all my baggage while cleaning horse shit, but it's not all bad. We are by the beach and it's the summer so there's a breeze and after each session, I go out to eat with my favorite fellow divorcée—Angelo (he's gay, unfortunately). We usually nosh at Nobu or the Malibu Country Mart. But lately, we started having picnics on the sand.

I pick a grape from Angelo's hand and throw it in my mouth. "You revealed a lot today."

Angelo smirks. "I love horses, what can I say. They really get me."

He takes another sip from his red plastic cup, lays on his back, and then drifts off. This happens each time—we feast on brioche, prosciutto, grapes, stone fruit, and gouda galore, and drink glass after glass of Grigio, and then he passes out. I am left all alone with nothing to do but read *The Cave,* this five-hundred-page romance novel about a Cro-Magnon woman who falls in love with a hunky Neanderthal. I bought it at the Malibu Country Mart from some discount book bin. Besides my therapist, the horses, and the Grigio, it has been the most consistent thing of my entire summer.

SO, I OPEN UP TO PAGE 103:

Grotta bent over and started skinning the fur off of the squirrel. The sun had begun to set. After peeling off the fur from the legs, she gathered some logs and started making her own fire. Minutes later, she was watching the squirrel roast on a spit, eagerly awaiting her dinner. Grotta didn't mind being alone. She would rather be in the cave than the village, where she'd be expected to gather berries or bake bread for the hunters.

From the distance, she heard a growl.
"GRRRRRRRRRRRRRR!"

Grotta turned around and there he was — Uluzzi, the hairy, brawny beast, was entering the cave. It had been five days since she had seen him last. Since he had helped her skin the fur off a squirrel. Since they almost kissed. Since they almost ignited another kind of fire.

Grotta whimpered. "Oh Uluzzi, I told you the hunters were on to you! I told you that after Cavallo caught his wife with one of yours, he threatened to destroy the last remnants of your kind."

Uluzzi ignored Grotta and started walking over to her. The embers of flame reflected off his thick brown fur, illuminating his uncanny aura.

"Oh Uluzzi."

He was tall and he was magnificent. He picked up the stick over the fire, took a bite of the finely burnt squirrel and then growled as blood dripped down his hairy neck.

"Oh Uluzzi!"

Grotta placed one hand on his shoulder and told him. "Uluzzi, let's just sit and have a meal. I want to give you pleasure. I want to give you my own feast."

Uluzzi made a barking sound and then followed Grotta's commands. She sat down after Uluzzi, slowly scooting towards him. The closer she got, the stronger his scent of sweat and soil. He took another bite of the squirrel— a burst of blood sprayed on her face, landing on her breasts and eager thighs.

"Oh Uluzzi!"

Grotta couldn't help it anymore. Moving with confidence, she bit into the squirrel. With the crisp meat hanging between her teeth and blood coating her lips, she leaned in and waited for Uluzzi to make the next move. He grasped the meat with his long, wet tongue, quickly masticating it before kissing her. She wrapped her arms around his trunk-like neck and passion overcame them. For she was his beauty and he was her ultimate fantasy — something untamable and yet eager to be desired, indifferent and yet complicit in mutual bliss.

Illustrations by Cassie Tucker

I watch Angelo as he sleeps. His long black hair is draped over his tanned forehead; a dollop of drool runs down his neck.

"Oh Angelo."

I put down *The Cave* and place my cup of Grigio on the sand. I walk towards the water, leaving Angelo and the picnic behind. Earlier that day at the stables, when I was cleaning shit while talking to my therapist about me cheating on Ricky at the lake house and him leaving and the night at Bootsy Bellows that ended with a totaled Mustang, the horse made the softest growl—the first time in weeks I got any kind of response from any of them.

My therapist then turned to me and said:

"CONGRATS. YOU'RE BOTH MAKING PROGRESS."

Illustrations by Cassie Tucker

SHOW CAVES

Austin Irving

 Carlsbad Caverns, Elevator Room, NM

SHOW CAVES is a collection of large format photographs that explores the anthropocentric tendencies of modern tourism seen in domestic and international show caves. Show caves are natural caves managed by government or commercial organizations that have been modified to accommodate tourism. The objective of this body of work is to highlight the tension that exists between the staggering natural beauty of caves and the renovations people make in order to transform these spaces into spectacular tourist attractions. These caverns have been curated to cater to both the physical needs of sightseers as well as to our collective expectation of the fantasy of a cave. Elaborate lighting, elevators, poured cement trails, even bathrooms and souvenir stands have been added so that ancient geological wonders can be accessible and marketable to a money giving public.

Are these additions acts of vandalism disrupting a delicate ecosystem for the sake of commercial profit? Or do these human interventions draw attention to the preservation of caves and make hard-to-access natural wonders readily available for appreciation?

 Howe Caverns, Narrow Path, NY

The images included in this series were made with a Toyo Field camera on 4x5 color negative on location in Singapore, Vietnam, Malaysia, New Mexico, Virginia, Arizona, New York and Tennessee.

Borra Caves, Light Cage, India

Shenandoah Caverns, Underground Phone, VA

27 Dau Go Gave Interior With Penguin Trash Cans, Vietnam

29 Borra Caves, Overlook, India

Colossal Cave, Display Case, NV

Shenandoah Caverns, Rainbow Lake, VA

 The Lost Sea, TN

Carlsbad Caverns, Employee Entrance, NM

AUSTIN IRVING

 Carlsbad Caverns, Souvenir Stand, NM

BORN AND RAISED IN NEW YORK CITY, Austin Irving graduated with a BFA from the Department of Photography and Imaging at TISCH School Of The Arts at New York University. Her artwork has been exhibited in galleries and museums internationally in Hong Kong, India and Paris and domestically in New York, California, Ohio, Washington, Illinois, Virginia and New Mexico. In 2016, she was a nominee for the United States Artists Fellowship and was a finalist in both the Architecture and Landscape categories for the Felix Schoeller Photo Award in Osnabrück, Germany. Her images have been featured in The LA Times, Wired, Slate, Architectural Digest, Art Ltd., Artillery, TimeOut NY, The International Herald Tribune, The Huffington Post, Frontrunner, Artsy, Yatzer, and Artweek LA.

Irving currently lives and works in Los Angeles and her work is represented by Wilding Cran Gallery.

NI PHO IN

IT TOOK TWO YEARS TO ACCEPT THAT THE CLUB I once called home doesn't exist for me anymore. The ominous concrete building that houses Output in Brooklyn's Williamsburg neighborhood, a stage for some of the best in House and Techno music, remains. My connection to it, on the other hand, is no longer.

Output opened its doors in January of 2013. At that time, I was beginning to skim the surface of the live scene through my explorations of dancemusic in the digital realm. A like-minded crew of my college friends and I spent our first night in this new space on March 31st of that year. When Robert Hood, one of the most respected names in Detroit Techno (the genre's origin city), came to Output that August, I was officially hooked.

A EULOGY FOR THE RAVE CAVE

The Output Years

2013
|
2015

Becca Van K

The subsequent two years were a flurry of excitement and anticipation. Every week was spent working to mentally prepare for my next Output night. Every dollar I earned was with the intention of spending it on train tickets to the city from upstate, club tickets, and drugs. I religiously checked the upcoming schedule, excitedly texting my club mates, Nate and Leila, about the next good show. A solid club partner provides support and trust, which I had, and still have, in these two. My rocks on the dance floor.

Photographs by Becca Van K

I made friends. I solidified existing relationships. Sneakers and a fanny pack became my uniform, for they were unparalleled in facilitating a marathon of dance. Amphetamine-driven cravings led me to smoke more cigarettes than I care to admit. I kissed a couple of strangers and friends. I befriended employees: Marcus, a friend of a friend who always tossed me a free water bottle with a wink; the stern West African man who guarded the bathrooms, who always yelled to me in French with a wry smile (forever a futile effort as the sound stormedin unapologetically from the next room). Somehow I still ended up with free candy.

I FELL IN LOVE WITH SOUND.

Output's policy on photography is explicit and well known: it is not allowed. The photos here breach that policy. These images (primarily video stills) are often the result of attempts to record songs I wanted to find post-show through digital channels. Every video is a whirlwind of flashing lights and darkness, broken up sporadically by a few frames of steady visuals. I have complicated feelings about their existence because I revere the space. Despite my periodic discomfort, they have become incredibly valuable to me, as the window of time between now and my experiences there grows larger. The memories in my mind are powerful, but none of them sent shivers up my spine or tears in my eyes like the act of listening to them again and seeing flashes of those nights.
I transport instantly.

House and Techno music demand personal dancing space. Pairs on the dance floor in a club of this type are few and far between—the code was well understood amongst the patrons. It is a truly unique experience to witness and express individual movement while simultaneously moving in sync with a whole group of people, and at Output, that privilege was not taken lightly. To feel both alone and entirely in tune with your surroundings, with the space and its people—it was a gift.

THE CROWDS THEN GOT LARGER

And with the more massive crowds and media popularity came the men who were there to meet women. On multiple occasions, men tried to take my personal space away from me. I no longer felt safe attending shows by myself. I felt anger and disappointment when I thought about the space, and that was wholly devastating. My time spent at Output, my club home, suddenly became past tense.

Photographs by Becca Van K

THE DANCE MUSIC WORLD EXISTED LONG BEFORE I TAPPED INTO THE SCENE, AND I CAN ONLY SPEAK TO MY OWN EXPERIENCE. IN RETROSPECT, I FEEL THAT I HAD ENTERED INTO THIS WORLD AT THE CREST OF A SIGNIFICANT SHIFT, CATCHING THE LAST COUPLE YEARS OF AN UNDERGROUND SCENE EDGING CLOSER AND CLOSER TO THE MAINSTREAM.

The House and Techno scene has exploded, fully inundating the broader cultural consciousness. The interest in this brand of dance music is positive in most ways, with the recognition of more female DJs (big up to Discwoman) and people of color (whose scene this was in the first place, explicitly queer people of color) in all corners of the world. It is undoubtedly exciting, but I feel like my head is spinning. Whereas five years ago, the NYC scene had ten parties on any weekend night, now there are thirty. Familiar club nights/ residencies grow larger, can cost up to $80, and even offer bottle service. It's frustrating to realize you are priced out, and disappointing to feel that places/nights you enjoyed and respected are forgetting their foundations (hello Cityfox). This is not to say that the underground is gone (in fact, it is flourishing), or that all parties are not reliable and financially accessible (thank you Mister Saturday Night, Bossa Nova Civic Club, Good Room,Mutual Dreaming,The Bunker, Unter). The scene grows, but the fact remains that deep down I feel somewhat divorced from a scene I once felt so close to.

For a time, Output became the main focus in my life—in some ways, a close friend. Since then, I've attended dozens of great parties at other clubs and warehouses, and I've seen some incredible DJs, but in truth, few of those nights paralleled my Output nights. I'm still on the mailing list,and I always feel a small twinge of desire when the newest lineup is announced. I toy with the idea of going, but I always decide against it...eventually. Writing about thisexperience forces me to acknowledge that the loss of Output still feels fresh. Man, was it something special.

HERE'S TO THE RAVE CAVE, MY CLUB HOME. I AM ENDLESSLY GRATEFUL.

With love. To Nate Gellman and Leila Bodeuil

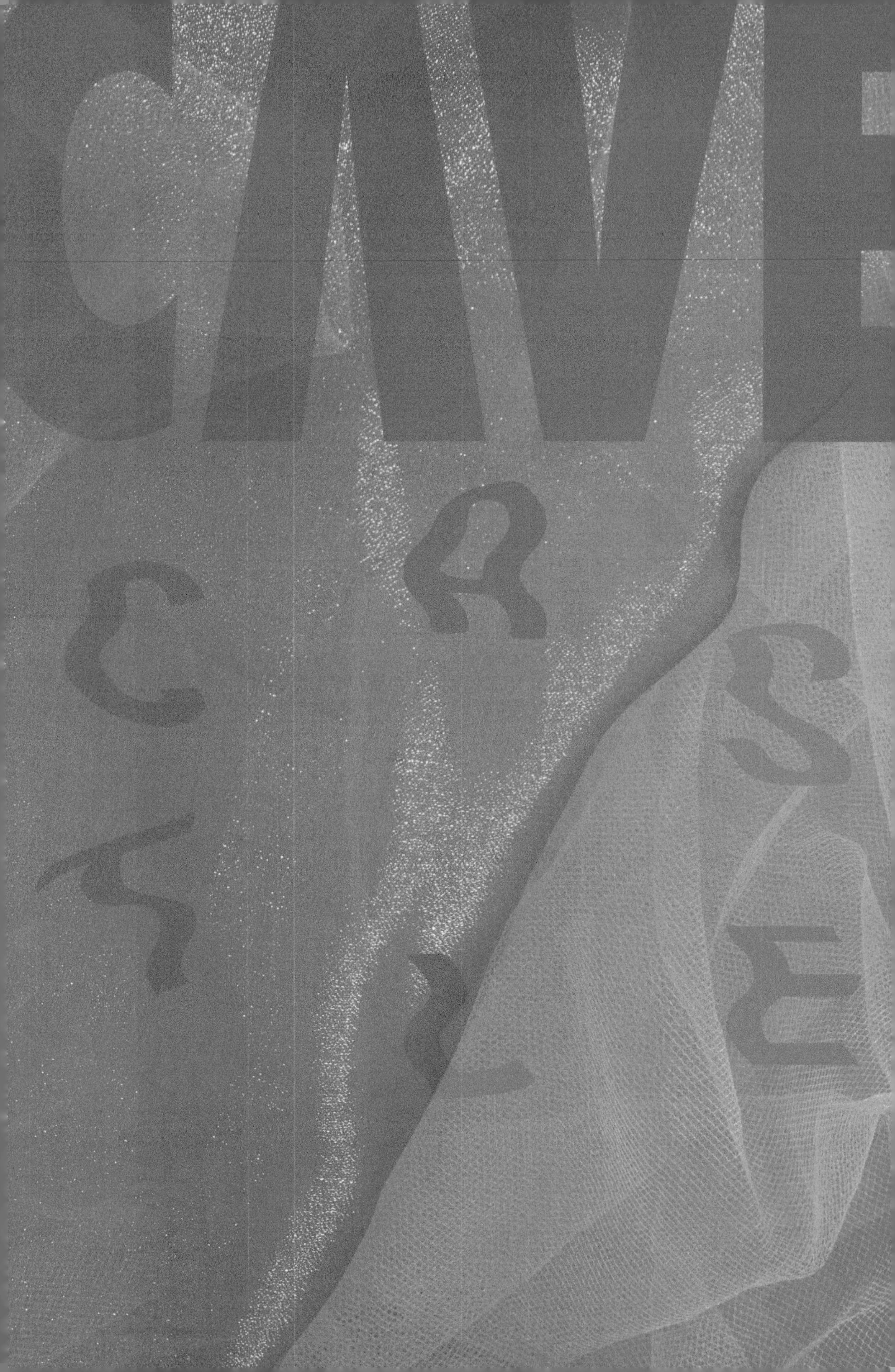
CAVE

AN OBSCURE PLACE

Hello Reading Friends,

I'm Dr. Nastya Valentine, CEO of Nastya Valentine Enterprises. You may know me from my product line, Nastya by Nastya Valentine Enterprises in collaboration with Nastya Valentine featuring Narc Jacobs sponsored by Red Bull paid for by Tesla and partially funded by The Boring Company, available at select Sephora stores and online at nastyavalentine.com where you could also shop a 20% off Ray Bans sale, HALF OFF designer handbags real Micheal Kors special edition cave spring for S/S 18 Paris Fashion Week NYFW use discount code: CAVE2018.

Aside from my branded content, you may know me from such films as *Day Drinkers: The Narrative: A Vampire Movie, Royal Girl Doing Relaxing Travel, Xanax 2, Party Castle Keynote Speech Executive Product Launch, and Fecking Movie.* What you may not know is that not only am I a filmmaker slash screenwriter slash thespian slash producer slash entrepreneur slash esthetician slash photographer slash brand ambassador slash writer slash dreamer, but I am also a slash hiker. Occasionally this sprightly polymath will be half a trail deep on a sunrise trek through Griffith Park when she discovers an obscure, never-before-seen grotto exquisitely placed near a subtropical median. Being as she is an inspired visionary, an apparition manifests to her of nuns huddling in this grotto upon an escape from their rigid convent; these sinister sisters use the cave as a place of patriarchy-free sinning, smoking, and eating candy after decades of fruitlessly serving the lord, confined to a diet of oatmeal and stale air. Three of them, with a crown on their fair hairs and a blunt in their hands. A synesthetic mirage drenched in Twizzlers and weed smoke. Settled immaculately amongst a dirty grotto, their beauty is ghostlike, almost princesslike. The inspired visionary is so moved by this experience that she calls a team together at once to produce a shoot that will so be enlightening to the niche community of liberated cave nuns that this lifestyle may well break out into the stream of acceptance in popular culture. The inspired visionary is concerned about connecting obscure communities and aesthetic experiences. She is a humanitarian. She is a provider. She is me.

Writing this, I am in my West Hollywood apartment daintily devouring a delicate lavender biscuit and critically examining caves, starting from the utopia cave nuns. Mom, I'm not emo anymore, I'm grotto grunge!!!! I'm thinking I'll use that narrative to further thematically develop my next high-concept palatial party slash art show slash immersive gallery experience, which may possibly slash probably be called Cave Castle. Tagline: an obscure place.

Historically, caves were places where religious and philosophical figures could do their job and help out the trajectory of the human non-corporeal timeline. Plato, I don't need to say anything. St. Thomas Aquinas, Alypius of the Caves, Kuksha of the Kiev Caves, and other servants of the divine had cloistered themselves in caverns, obscured from all. Zen monks lived in caves to protect from the elements and evade the government. Early man is called the caveman. Descartes had locked himself in an oven for three days and had visions that resulted in Cartesian math today as we know it. Not a cave per se, but the oven seems to serve a similar function. Nestor the Chronicler, an Eastern Orthodox scribe, lived up to his name and chronicled Anthony of Kiev and Theodosius of the Caves, two more saintly cavemen. Even a Google search of "monks in caves" pulls up a Wikipedia page of "List of Cave Monasteries." Cavewomen of the religious or historical kind are more difficult to encounter. Where are the cave nuns? The cloistered sisters of the lord or the merciless wenches of the hail satin? My Google searches for "religious women in caves," "nuns in caves," "historical cavewomen," etc., turned out pathetically empty, save for a "Cave Lady of Las Vegas" urban legend. Not as fruitful as the detailed "List of Cave Monasteries."

One of the items in the fruitful list, Pechersky Ascension Monastery in Nizhny Novgorod, Russia, I had actually been to the previous summer. The Russian word for cave is peschera. There is a surprising amount of Russian historical figures associated with caves, a fact that as a Russian slash cave lover I'm happy to learn about. I try to method-curate my work as much as possible, and points of personal connection help string me along the path. Connection and organization is my shit. I'm obsessed with taxonomy.

I'm obsessed with nomenclature and compulsive organization. I'm obsessed with obsession. And my Castles are my children; they are high-concept art parties that start like this in some dump of a Microsoft Word .docx and end up becoming palatial gallery installations. My fine artist, musician, fashion designer, DJ, engineer, and scientist friends contribute their art in an inclusive environment underscored by a specific theme.

The next Castle, the aforementioned one to be called Cave Castle, is going to be utopia-themed. That is without question the trajectory. The utopian nun grotto of an indeterminate timeline. I believe the name of the Castle contributes to its destiny. This one is the fourth installment. After a dramatic planning for the dystopia-themed Nuclear Castle, a hazy planning for celestial spa resort Space Castle, and a drug fuelled gonzo bender for vaporwave mall Party Castle, I'm ready to steer the self-fulfilling prophecy into calm waters and rapturous utopias.

Let us psychologically spelunk into the abyss. The disruption present in the timeless void of feckless infinite space, let me tell you… feckless is a real word, as confirmed by the Webster dictionary. Emotionally preparing oneself to enter the cave, one must not be feckless but rather fearless. Remember that as one of their traditionally defining features, caves go deep.

The caver's state of mind should be mimetic of a cave: no therapist should come out of there the same, physically or emotionally. Your cave should resemble David Blaine's personality, which is actually David Lynch, which is actually a cave.

DIFFERENCES BETWEEN DAVID BLAINE AND A LUNCHABLE:

1 of them can escape from a cube,
the other one can give young children
amphetamine psychosis;

1 of them is an award-winning magician,
the other one works in Las Vegas;

1 of them comes in a plastic container,
the other one was popular in the 90s;

1 of them is an endurance artist,
the other one endures hours of agony
being digested in a small intestine;

1 of them is David Lynch, the other
one is also David Lynch;

1 of them has a family and children,
the other one feeds a family and
children;

differences between david blaine
and a lunchable is...... there is
no difference!!!!!

ONE OF THEM CAN BE PURCHASED AT A 7-11...

BLAINE JOKES WORKSHOP

No one knows how inspiration strikes. No one also knows how caves work.

At Cave Castle, assuming this is the direction we are going in now, visitors will be greeted by an artisanal boxed lunch that can survive in a subterranean environment, inspired by space food and containing vacuum sealed bags of luxury snacks and emergency water. This version of cosmonaut cuisine is not only nutritious, but presented in a sexy packaging. As you know, presentation is everything. There will be a VIP dining cavern for the best geologists in the field, djed by Geologist from Animal Collective.

The décor of the cave will follow one of my favorite movements, the rococo style. No Lascaux kindergarten bullshit. Luscious florals, extravagant crystal patterns, gold plated vanity mirrors, sky-high powdered wigs, romantic fainting couches everywhere. Ladies, gentlements, everyone in between, do pair a hoop skirtframe with your Adidas. You will get to feel like a very stylish and exclusive hermit.

LET THEM EAT CAVE. LET THEM LISTEN TO VIVALDI REMIXES.

It is common to go into a cave and hear ethereal music. Less common is doing a gram of molly and DJing a private cave, or putting contact mics on stalactites and finding out what sounds they make. Such acoustic experiments are rare but nonetheless add a sparkle to the breadth of things that can transform a cave interior.

Will there be a DJ at Cave Castle getting brick faced and encouraging casual drug use on property, or a string quintet atmospherically taming the vibes? Unpopular opinion, but caves remain the chillest places to do drugs and listen to music.

Caves are incredibly diverse. Freudian dream interpretation suggests that caves can be anything from a *physical-psychological-psychosomatic-psychotomimetic-pseudosexual* exploration of a new place, to a return to the maternal womb, to a symbol of the reality beyond "this" reality, the one that rich billionaires are paying scientists shitloads of money to hack into. If you haven't been sold on caves yet, my friends, my family, remember: a cave is the best place to hide from a dystopia.

Ten Things Worse Than an Eleven Day Raging Drug Bender in a Cave:

- cheating on your veganism
- not getting a facial every four to six weeks
- the dentist
- taylor swift
- 5
- my instagram story
- number 6 will SHOCK you
- students loans
- u2 showing up in itunes unannounced and you cant get rid of it >[
- when you go on a first date with a dude or a second date or something and he doesn't know animal collective beyond mpp and my girls and you hate yourself for being judgeymental but youre trying to do laundry with him anyway but he's quiet and awkward and not showing any interest in you or animal collective or glamour or more critically it seems like he doesn't want to do laundry so you lock yourself in a cave for a week and a half working on one of kaney's unreleased track but protools crashed so you lost all the track datas and now not only some random dude doesn't want to do laundry with you but kaney is gonna be really pissed and have another mental breakdown that is all your fault that the album is stalling so you buy a fainting couch for the fainting cave with the advance that you were planning to pay off your student loans with so you are back to square one but you relate to Kanye in that way right because we all have debts right it's human conditioner so you guess you'll go to the opera after your bender cause that's so on brand reminding yourself that some things should be better left alone and accept that accenptance is key to living gracefully but technically drugs are a form of grace and the year you spent being completely sober was a strange branding activity and possible waste of time and conclude that there should definitely more caves because caves help you "self-deprecate and create" or "deteriorate and meditate" or whatever
- feet

Photographs by Charlie Hawks

Mine, Ben

WHITE

MAN

IN A

HOLE

THE CENTRAL THEME IN THE PORTFOLIO "KUPA-PITI: WHITE MAN IN A HOLE," IS THE SEEMING ABSURDITY IN LIFE.

This series has been made in a small town named Cooper Pedy, in the middle of the Australian desert, also referred to the opal capital of the world. Many of its first inhabitants were migrants from southern and eastern Europe after the Second World War in search of the precious Opal-stone. Due to the sandstorms and the harsh summer temperatures they built their homes into the mines. The Aboriginals describe this phenomenon with the term Kupa-piti witch translates to 'white man in a hole'.

Today, in a world where science and technology are reaching new peaks, these fortune seekers still live like cavemen. You have the impression that these people are trying to escape something, that the mine is a retreat that is detached from reality. To live in total isolation to find a rock - it's the raw reality that dreams can be reduced to it. It is the confrontation with extreme banality. Can you stop, can you still get back?

Is this the eternal return of Nietzsche, or the existentialist myth of Sisyphus, which represents the absurdity of life? Is the goal of finding these precious stones inherently meaningless? Is the challenge faced by these people to refrain from despair?

Or should we consider Albert Camus' conclusion in his essay "The Myth of Sisyphus" that, "one must imagine Sisyphus happy."

Matthias Van Dromme

BEDFORD

MATT
HIAS

VAN

DRO
MME

 Phil's Dugout, New Home

Matthias Van Dromme (1988, Mechelen) is a photographer based in Ghent, Belgium. He graduated in 2011 with a BA in Photography at School of Arts, Ghent, Belgium. KUPA-PITI: White Man in a Hole (2017) is his first finished work.

THE DARK RECESSES OF THE FOURTH HOUSE:

CAVERNS, OCEANS AND EMOTIONAL WELLS

Wade Caves

Most of us only have exposure to the world of astrology through our Sun signs. For example, birthdays occurring between May 20 to June 20 will have the Sun in Gemini, and the familiar traits of that sign shine through: an inclination toward talkativeness, an inquisitive and curious mind, a youthful quality (note that Gemini is the sign of the two pre-pubescent twins) which can sometimes manifest as hesitance to commit.

But the signs and the planets are only two layers in a complex astrological puzzle. The real magic in astrology comes from the houses, divisions of the sky both above and below the horizon which help to locate where in life the planetary activity will be felt or enacted. For instance, the eastern horizon marks the center of the first house. As the Sun rises here each day, this area of the sky speaks to life, health, vitality and the body of someone born. The western horizon captures that person's opposing forces: enemies, lovers, business partners and the immediate outside environment. This is the seventh house.

The Sun's point of culmination in the southern skies (where the Sun is roughly at noon) is the center of the tenth house, a house associated with the height of success, achievement, and industry. However, the fourth house, the point exactly opposite to the tenth, is thrust under the earth. As this house is below the horizon, it is shielded from our view, and is considered dark and hidden. The fourth house is where the Sun passes through around midnight: it is below us, the most submerged area of the astrological chart (often called 'subterranean' in Greek texts).

The symbolism of the fourth house is very much connected to the fact that it is removed from our view and is found well beneath the earth. This house governs our ancestral lineage, a tangible link to our history and past. It also rules our home and property, or in other words, the ground beneath our feet. But a more curious and fascinating connection exists between the fourth house and oceans, deep waters, caverns and barren landscapes.

Each planet is said to rejoice in certain houses, houses which share similar meanings or have similar dispositions or outlooks. Jupiter, for example, is a joyful and jubilant planet, and rejoices in the eleventh house of friends, benefactors, ambition and hope. The meanings of the houses are often derived from the planets associated with that house.

Today's astrologers would say that the planet Saturn – a cold and dry planet which reflects very little light back to us here on Earth, and often has a depressive energy – finds his joy in

the twelfth house of secret enemies, isolation and self-undoing. But one author writing before the system of house joys was canonised put Saturn to the fourth house. To this day, the fourth carries a strong Saturnian feel. Marcus Manilius wrote in his 1st century AD astrological poem Astronomica that this house has strong associations with the planet Saturn, the god of time:

> WHERE AT THE OPPOSITE POLE THE UNIVERSE SUBSIDES, OCCUPYING THE FOUNDATIONS, AND FROM THE DEPTHS OF MIDNIGHT GLOOM GAZES UP AT THE BACK OF THE EARTH, IN THAT REGION [VIS-À-VIS, THE FOURTH HOUSE] SATURN EXERCISES THE POWERS THAT ARE HIS OWN: CAST DOWN HIMSELF IN AGES PAST FROM EMPIRE IN THE SKIES AND THE THRONE OF HEAVEN, HE WIELDS AS A FATHER POWER OVER THE FORTUNE OF FATHERS AND THE PLIGHT OF THE OLD. DAEMONIUM IS THE NAME THE GREEKS HAVE GIVEN [THIS HOUSE], DENOTING INFLUENCING FITTING THE NAME.[1]

For Manilius, the fourth house carries these themes of old age, history, and family lineage (fathers in particular) due to its association with the slowest visible planet, Saturn. This is a sector of the sky which plunges downward, connecting to the image of depth and submersion. The fourth's association with caves is a telling one: caverns are dark and devoid of natural light, bore into the more infertile regions of the earth, and are not conducive to natural life (which may be why they provide such great shelter from outside threats – a very Saturnian kind of protection). In my studies, I have come across one chart which is particularly poignant: it was cast to locate the whereabouts of a missing person feared dead. The chart showed that the missing person was dead and had gone missing as a result of dementia. With a strong fourth house emphasis in this chart, it was unsurprising that the deceased person was found near a cave.

Similarly, the great expanse of the ocean brings in a sense of seclusion and loneliness. The high salt content of ocean water is inhospitable to human life,[2] invoking the image of Saturn as the natural ruler of death and the grave. In the early 1900s, New York City astrologer Evangeline Adams was on trial for predictions she made for clients as a consulting astrologer. In her trial, she defended her work and insisted on demonstrating her skill for the court to counter any charges of wrongdoing. She was given birth chart data (birth time, place, location) of an anonymous person and given a few minutes to make a relevant pronouncement. She described this person for the court as having striking physical features, but a sad and difficult

life, one marked by tension with parents (a fourth house theme). Her clever use of certain fourth house signatures in this anonymous chart allowed her to make the salient point that this person's life would be cut short, saying she saw a tragic event and a 'watery, watery grave'. The court fell silent as the judge announced in a sombre tone that the birth data she had been given was that of the judge's own son, who had just recently drowned. He then dismissed the case, clearing Adams of all charges, saying that she 'raised astrology to the dignity of an exact science.'

While common associations with the fourth house are dark and often incorporate images of the grave (or of burying), this house need not be so literal. The connections to caves and deep places in the earth are both literal and symbolic. People born with strong fourth house themes will have deeply embedded values, often those which escape the active, conscious acknowledgement of the native. Venus in the fourth, for instance, often speaks to those who have a tremendous well of emotion, and are strongly motivated by the forming of relationships and the pursuit of a lasting love. Mars in this house often shows someone with a deep reserve of friction and anger, or at the very least a continuous source for onward movement. They will be propelled and motivated by frustration more than they recognise themselves.

Planets can also contribute to the affairs of this house without being placed within them. Those with Jupiter forming a harmonious aspect to the cusp of the fourth house need homes and private places that are filled with light, boast plenty of moving air, and provide a great sense of relief and release. The Moon or Sun aspecting the fourth cusp will do much the same, particularly where the need for light is concerned.

The fourth house is a meaningful house, one of four which mark the 'angles' or 'pivots' of the astrological scheme. Rich with astrological insight, astrologers use the connections to this house to understand the symbolic caves and oceans within us all, the ways in which we tend to bury what we would rather not have exposed, and how we work with energies that form the foundations beneath our very own feet. Often, simple acknowledgement of what is churning us from underneath is all we need to move forward in our lives in a more conscientious and meaningful way.

---

[1] Manilius, Astronomica, 2. 929-938. Loeb edition, p. 157. 1977. Additions/alterations in brackets are mine, to facilitate easier understanding.

[2] Contrast this with the Dead Sea, a sea so salty that no natural life can grow or develop there (hence its name).

GRAYLORB

THE SPIDER LICH
ENCHANTED SORCERER OF THE GREAT CAVE IN THE TANGLED SHREDWOOD

The entity who wears the mask of Graylorb was once a master spell caster, revered by his fellow cultists. On a dark quest through the Tangled Shredwood he was met by a huge and malevolent spider. The Spider gave Graylorb the choice of being enslaved or being enchanted by the soul of a spider lich. In his panicked state he chose enchantment and opened his mind and body to the wretched lich. In doing so he has become a phantom of his former self, hiding in the mouth of a great cave during the day and terrorizing the realm under the light of the moon. The Graylorb that was once a revered sorcerer now desperately lives to serve the whims of the jaded lich within.

To find out more about Graylorb and a whole array of cultish creatures, check out Michael Koehler's website: MRKOEHLER.COM and be sure to follow him on Instagram: @LORDOFTHEFJORD to stay updated on the world of the Cult Realms!

●●●○○WT&F
9:52 PM
60%
3
From: Me
To:
GET PAID
Today at 9:30 PM
By Lux.

He needed to get away from his family. Visits had been tough since his mom married Greg, the guy who teaches smithing classes at the warehouse near the bridge. The house still smelled like smoke, but the sharpness of charcoal had replaced the musty implication of cigarettes. There was only so much Murder She Wrote he could watch with Greg hammering away in the garage.

It's not that the trips home were unpleasant, exactly. They were grating. It was a slow process. Excitement became tolerance, which became boredom, which became irritation, which became an insatiable desire to get the fuck away from them and back to his real life.

Real life was spinning a reputation earned by a few pieces of long-form college journalism into sponsored content about gaming computers and electric razors. He'd get away from the forging and the Angela Lansbury and step into a studio apartment with a mouse, an air mattress, and a pile of bills and rejection letters.

So that's how he ended up on a steep hill facing the Western Pennsylvania woods. He lit another cigarette and got back to writing in his notebook. It was another story about the history of the internet. The New Yorker was supposed to love this kinda shit. As long as he kept banging his head against this particularly pretentious wall, he'd eventually get through. Then he could be on staff somewhere. People would follow him on Twitter. Maybe Laura from the year he spent at that MFA program would text him back.

It was quiet. That was his favorite thing about taking a break from Philadelphia. It was easy for him to get lost in his work. He turned to a new page and lit a fresh cigarette. The scratch of his pencil cut through the soft whisper of wind through the trees.

It wasn't long before he put the pencil down, pulled out his phone, and started checking emails, and then comparing follower counts with people from his high school class and lingering perhaps overly long on his ex's photographs from her recent trip to Palau. He'd read about halfway through a thread on journalism's latest moral failure when a twig snapped liked thunder.

His head snapped around, and in the moonlight, he could see it. Hunched over to avoid low hanging branches was a vast body, bulging with muscle. Yellow eyes glistened like diner eggs over a mouth made for chomping through bones. Hair hung unevenly from its bulbous head in thick, lanky strands. It took a step toward him into a puddle of light. Now he could see its tusks and pale grey skin.

He snatched up his phone, his lighter, and his notebook and he kicked up dust. His attempt at scrambling away was thwarted when he tripped and tumbled forward onto his chest. He rolled over to look back and it was staring at him. It raised its hands and started to bark. It was a deep sound. Something from a dark place where native species have evolved without eyes. For the first time in his life, he wished he had one of Greg's homemade swords.

It wasn't approaching. It was just making that sound and shaking. It lowered its hands to its knees, rumbling like a garbage truck.

"Are you laughing at me?!" He didn't mean to say it, but he wasn't about to be judged by whatever the hell this thing was. He was a writer, goddamnit! He went to fucking school. Who the fuck was this Elephant Man knock off to laugh at him?

"Of course I am. You tripped and fell on your butt. How could I not laugh? You fell. Right on your butt."

"You scared me!"

"Oh because I look a little weird?"

"No. Off course not. You just surprised me is all." The thing started rumbling again. "Stop laughing at me!" In one lumbering motion, it was inches from his face. He could smell rotting meat, swamp water, and dirt. So much dirt.

"I don't scare you, little snack? You know, back before you soft bodies found cold iron you'd be an hors-d'oeuvres. I'd eat your fingers and toes, feed the rest to my kids, and then move on to a real meal. Your bones would sit with a thousand others at the bottom of a dark hole. Back then you wouldn't dare come out here.

You'd be too scared of me, of the idea of me, to shit out your magnum opus under the oak tree. Don't lie to me, little human. I can smell it."

It stepped away, and he finally exhaled.

"Okay but you're not going to eat me, right?"

"Like what?"

IT SIGHED.

"NO. NO, I'M NOT. I CAN'T DO THAT. YOU GO MISSING. THEY START LOOKING. THEN THE GUNS COME OUT. NO THANK YOU.THERE ARE EASIER WAYS TO GET ALONG THESE DAYS."

"Well, funny you should ask. That's why I'm here. See, I heard you out here, and I took a little sniff and recognized the smell. I lived here when you were a kid, so I gave it a Google." He cocked an eyebrow, and it pulled a battered iPhone out from the leather strap around its waist. It shrugged. "You find all kinds of things where people aren't looking. Anyway, I poked around the old information superhighway and stumbled across your work. I was stunned. The little boy who used to imagine fantastical adventures in my woods was out in the world writing such wonderful things. I thought to myself, you know I might have some work for a guy like that."

"Work?" His ears perked up. Whether from a subscription footcare company or a mysterious beast, when work calls, you have to answer the phone.

"Yeah well, think about it. I'm a TROLL. A real-life cave troll. Distant relative of the one from Moria--"

"Really?"

"No. Just because Trolls are real doesn't mean Middle Earth is. Where do you think Tolkien got the idea?"

Illustrations by May Parsey

"Folktales, right?"

"Folktales based on true events! And that question was rhetorical, by the way."

"Right, sorry. So the job?"

"Someone needs to tell my story! I'm big news! I'll do an interview, a photo shoot, the whole shebang. I want the world to know about me, but I'm not exactly a wordsmith, and honestly, I can't type with these sausage fingers."

"So you want me to ghostwrite your coming out announcement?"

"Yes! That's exactly what I want. Well said! This is why you're the writer."

"Ok...sure, so I compose this expose, and you pay me what?" The smile dropped off the Troll's face. It sighed.

"I don't have much. Rocks, trash, broken things. This phone's my most valuable asset, and well...it ain't much. I guess you'd just be writing for the exposure on this one."

Exposure. Unpaid labor. The modus operandi of a society that turns everyone with even a fractional spark of creativity into an idea factory for faceless corporations.

"Sorry. No deal. I don't work for free."

"This is a big opportunity though. We put this out, people will see it."

"Why don't we just sell the story somewhere? Then you can pay me with some of that money."

"Sell the story?? No way! Once this breaks, we'll be licensing the rights nonstop! Printing money! You just need to write it, get it out there, and then wait, and once that pops off, you'll be HUGE. J.D. Salinger huge, Philip Roth huge, J.K. Rowling huge."

"Assuming anyone believes it's real."

"Someone will at least follow-up to see! It'll grow, and it'll go viral. Viral!"

He should have said no. Years spent creating a veneer of self-respect told him to say no. Fair labor practices told him to say no, and he fancied himself the kind of person who cared about that sort of stuff.

And yet, something gave him pause. It was a feeling he had in his stomach; a feeling that he was in the middle of something real, something incredible. He'd felt it when he'd picked up the thread of any great story he'd written. He was feeling it on that hill. Shivering in front of a giant with an elephant's skin and his uncle's sense of humor, he felt it.

He saw the world fall into a montage. The story flowing from his fingers onto the internet. The article opening on phones, computers, even in the lenses of the last ten people wearing Google Glass. People asking for interviews. Himself and the troll on the news. The book deal to follow. The checks. The yacht. The apartment in Brooklyn. All of it...just a few thousand words away.

HE SHOULD HAVE SAID NO.

"I'll do it." The granite face split into a smile.

"Perfect! Perfect! Follow me. I'll introduce you to my family, we'll take some pictures, some video, then you get it out there, and we're good to go." The troll lumbered down the hill, and he scampered to keep up.

They made their way through the woods behind the house. They went off the path, into a thick wall of trees. They went down a ravine, up a hill, around a massive rock he'd never seen before, and into a tunnel.

Away from his mother. Away from the moon and the stars. Away from the familiar suburban streets, the cookie cutter houses and Greg's forge. They marched down, down, down.

It was dark when they stopped. The air smelled like old trash and farts. He flicked his lighter. It sparked but didn't catch. The troll grabbed his arm. "Don't do that. You'll scare them."

"Who?"

"My family." The troll started rumbling. The cave shook. He could hear movement. Huge shapes shifting, rising in the dark.

"So, can I turn on the light? Are we ready for interviews?" He thought about a yacht and a residency somewhere that paid him to do nothing.

"I think so." He fiddled with his phone, and the flashlight came on.

He didn't have time to count the trolls before the first one grabbed his leg. Another grabbed his arm. He screamed. "You have to respect yourself more. You're a good writer kid, but you can't just give it away like that." The troll started laughing again. He screamed. Something started chewing.

At the top of the hill, Greg put away his hammer and tongs and headed upstairs to see his wife. They went to bed and didn't realize anything was wrong until the morning. The cops never found anything.

Illustrations by May Parsey

BRONSON CAVES

Brice Bischoff

THE BRONSON CAVES are located in Los Angeles' Griffith Park and are famous as a filming location to countless motion pictures and television shows. Early after their creation in 1903 as excavation routes for a quarry company, movie studios began renting the site for filming. The caves' cinematic history begins here and continues to the present day. Over the course of this history, the caves are documented as an unchanging landscape amidst a chaotic specter of fictional realities. Cinema has imaged events from explosions and gunfights to the creation of cave paintings and alien abductions at the Bronson Caves. With each cinematic event the landscape's existence morphs and adapts to new realities, an asteroid colony one event, a vampire lair the next. The site is a truly unique and relatively unknown American landscape.

In the series of photographs titled Bronson Caves, I am attempting to photograph the caves's extensive cinematic history in one moment, collapsing space and time.
To do this I meditated on all the millions of movements and actions recorded by cinema at the caves, and I performed for the camera with massive sheets of colored paper. Since a long-exposure photograph was produced rather than a motion picture, the papers were recorded as voluminous, glowing colors. The paper was transformed, and the materiality of the rainbowed forms, emerging from the mouth of the cave, dancing about the canyon, and bubbling up from the ground, are based solely in the photographic process, which can only be experienced when viewing the final photographic images. If a visitor to the caves were to accidently stumble upon my performance they would only see a mass of crumbled colored paper draped awkwardly over a man moving/dancing to a camera positioned on a tripod.

THE GOAL OF MY PERFORMANCES AND ULTIMATLEY THE PHOTOGRAPHS WERE TO CREATE SCULPTURAL, PHOTOGRAPHIC OBJECTS THAT INTERACT WITH THE HISTORY AND ARCHITECTURE OF THE CAVES.

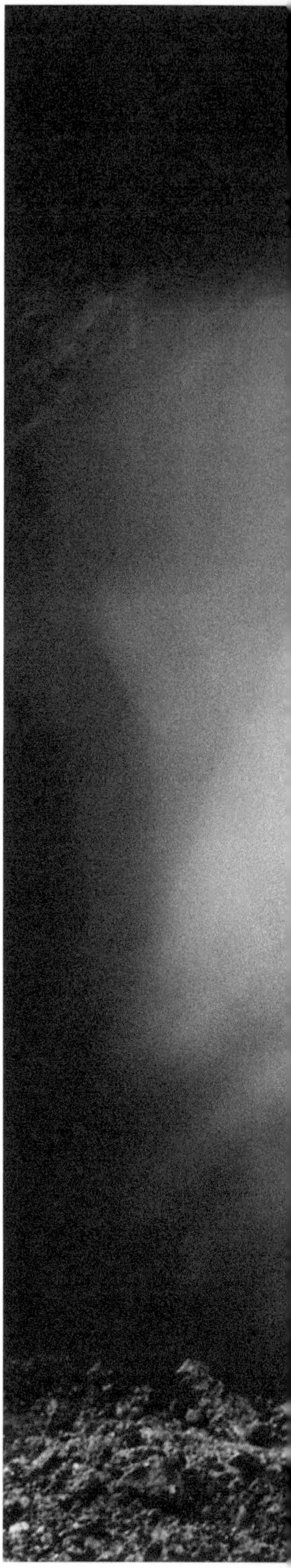

BRICE BISCHOFF

Brice Bischoff is an artist based in Los Angeles who works primarily with photography. His work questions the logic of photographic representation, light and space, and the reality of objects/place.

He is represented by Cirrus Gallery, Los Angeles and his work is in the collections of the Los Angeles County Museum of Art and the Orange County Museum of Art among others. His work has recently been in exhibitions at the MAK Center, Los Angeles, the Orange County Museum of Art and a solo show at a l m projects in the Hollywood Hills.

BURIED CULTURES:

A SHORT GENEALOGY OF THE CHEESE "CAVE"

Jessica Merliss

The cave-aged cheese, ripening and blooming within the inner-sanctum of a mysterious subterranean space, is a romantic image we have clung to for centuries. This is in part because we are taught to refer to fermentation chambers as caves. After milk is cultured and rennet applied, cheese curds are pressed into molds to drain any lingering whey, and then placed in the cave and left to ripen.[1] However, when we talk of cheese caves, we are in actuality referring to artificial spaces designed to mimic certain natural characteristics of the cave. A ripening room must be impenetrable to undesirable microbes, or in other words, sealed off from the outside world, but it must also be able to sustain the microbial populations that work symbiotically to construct pleasurable flavors, aromas, and textures in the product. For these reasons, "caves" are dark, temperature and humidity controlled spaces. At times, the unpredictable ripening process is monitored by affineurs[2]—aging specialists—to ensure the cheese successfully matures and reaches peak-flavor before getting tagged for distribution.

When delving into the history of these subterranean ripening rooms, what's curious is that cheese has never actually been aged in caves, but rather in grottos. Even the first cheesemakers to utilize caves had to augment them to accommodate their products. By turning the natural space into an artificial one, cheesemakers could both safeguard their products from detrimental fluctuations in the natural world, as well as expose their products to an unseen microbial population which highlights the unique terroir.

According to Jessica Sennett, cheese entrepreneur and historian, the grotto is a term used throughout history to designate what was often a man-made enclave reserved for

Photographs by Charlie Hawks

religious ceremony. The Italian word, grotto, is derived from the Latin word cropta (related to crypta), meaning vault, cavern, or hidden place. The French, on the other hand, derive the word from grotesque, which was often used to describe ancient Roman cave paintings. Of most interest to the query of this paper is the English meaning of the word grotto, which is simply an underground cave. This modified definition may explain why in the English language we have blurred the line between grottos and caves. Yet this does not fully satisfy the cheese cave dilemma, because Europeans aging cheese in grottos have referred to them as caves for centuries. With this in mind, we can conclude that cheeses were never aged in natural caves as our linguistic choice implies, but rather in cave-like environments outfitted with technology enabling total control of the space.

With the advent of electricity, the ambient cellars used for cheese fermentation became a technology of the past, and all the action moved above ground. Refrigerated cooling units enabled factories to increase their output of product so they could meet an increasing consumer demand. The Journal of Dairy Science (2017) indicates the first factory cheeses that were made in the United States were New York Cheddars in 1851, and along with the other cheese to follow in this era, they were usually cloth-bound, greased with fat or wax, and ripened on wooden shelves. With commercial refrigeration and the use of pasteurized milk, cheese factories have come close to eliminating the possible presence of known contaminants which could lead to potential public health catastrophes.

In contemporary times, these massive refrigeration units (which a dairy corporation like Tillamook owns) are less commonly the aging location for respected American-made cheeses. Most artisanal cheese-makers age their products in small-batches in what one might call a retrofitted refrigerator: one that is hacked to give the user control of the humidity and temperature. Some cheesemakers prefer to cling to the romantic ideal of the pastoral dairy, aging their cheeses in highly technological environments designed to look like caves or subterranean vaults, as they do at Jasper Hill, one of the more notable American artisanal creameries. An even smaller amount still age their cheeses in actual grottos, like Fairbault Dairy in Minnesota, a tradition started by Felix Frederickson in 1936, when he expanded the caves so he could exclusively age his blue cheeses within them. But even these natural enclosures have been altered and expanded to accommodate the growing demand for this sublime ferment. Excavators drill into cave walls, manipulating the rock for their corporate benefit, and in doing so, ironically grow the lore of the space's underground mysteries.

The drive to assert control over the natural is not only visible in man's alteration of subterranean environments for fermentation production, but also in our attempts to actually ferment. Fermentation is a chemical (or even alchemical) process humans utilize to preserve food long past freshness, an obvious advantage in pre-modern agricultural societies. Once produce is harvested from the Earth, it begins to ripen, and eventually it rots. However, through fermentation, a stage that occurs in fruits

---

[1] Ripening refers to the process of sealing and aging fresh cheese in a climate-controlled environment which promotes specific microbial activity while limiting others. It is at this stage that the cheese may develop mold blooms, or take on any number of characteristics based on its interaction with the microbes in a specific environment. Cheese may be ripened for anywhere from two weeks to several years long, and wheels are usually stored on wooden slats to promote and strengthen the desirable microbe populations, and to control humidity.

[2] Affineurs determine when wheels of cheese are ready to be sold, and some have oddly supernatural ways of performing their craft. I was once told a story about a Parmesan affineur (a post of very high standing) who was known in the industry for his habit of talking to his cheeses. He told people that the cheeses would whisper to him, and when they were ready to come off the shelf they would tell him. That was truly his method—pure instinct based on magical thinking.

naturally between states of ripe and rotted, man is able to intervene. He can slow this process down so that produce may be viable for a longer period of time. When fermenting dairy, a cheesemaker introduces the bacterial culture Lactobacillus to the milk which digests and converts lactose–the milk sugar–into lactic acid, a natural preservative that prevents the growth of harmful bacterias. This allows the curds to dry and age without spoiling.

Throughout the history of civilization, countless cultures have utilized fermentation processes to sustain themselves during winters and scarce hunting seasons. Some argue the first people to settle down into agrarian communities did so to grow wheat for the brewing of ale. These ferments, even today, serve as cultural designators internationally, with countries like Korea known for its kimchi and makgeolli; Spain for its charcuterie and orujo; Germany for its sauerkraut and kolsch. But even though we prize these foods as national treasures, some might liken them more closely with garbage. A non-scientific, literary way to frame the fermentation process would be through an allusion to a story like Poe's "The Facts in the Case of M. Valdemar." In it, a 19th century doctor who aspires to loftiness in a reckless kind of Faustian way, pursues a sick mesmeric experiment where he sustains his terminal friend Monsieur Valdemar in a trance just before the moment of his death. His body dies and begins to degrade, but his soul or essence or consciousness is still stuck within the body, alive and well. What happened to Valdemar, sustained in a prolonged phase between life and death, speaking with a raspy, guttural and altogether different voice—that is fermentation.

We are taught from a young age to avoid eating bread with moldy blue spots, but when we are served a cheese plate, we are then, mind-bogglingly enough, told to eat and even savor the mold. Horrible smells likened to feet, farts, cat piss, horse shit, and garlic corpse (don't ever let 10 gallons of kimchi sit undisturbed in a hundred degree kitchen for two months) occur regularly, and in certain cases, those can be highly desirable qualities. Is it not strangely coincidental that the same revulsions provoked by a ferment are also provoked by the cave?

To answer this question it is important to first understand some of the intuitive meanings conveyed through the cave throughout social history and popular culture. The cave is a place unimaginably vast and threatening, but it has also always offered itself as shelter to the lost and weary. For both Plato and Francis Bacon, the cave is a site characterized by its ability to bestow or bury knowledge of the past. What drives a polarizing wedge between these two thinkers is a matter of directional logic. For Plato, the enlightened philosopher on a true quest for knowledge leaves the shadowy cave,

Photographs by Charlie Hawks

illuminated only by flames, to ascend into the natural world—his eyes acclimating to the light as more time is spent basking in its glory. On the other hand, Bacon felt that the search for true knowledge insisted people descend into the caves, showering them with artificial, electrical light in the hopes of unburying the secrets of modern civilization. Their eyes, too, must slowly acclimate, but this time, to the darkness so they may relearn what has been forgotten over time. In both cases, the pursuit of knowledge is what saves us from a feeling of powerlessness in the face of our impending doom, but it is also dually the catalyst of our inevitable demise.

Journeying across time, the cave, as it appears in literature, poetry and painting in the 19th century, is central to the imagery of the sublime. Edmund Burke explains the sublime is our response to the tension between action and contemplation. He equates this expectation with the feeling animals have when they hear a slight noise and prick their ears up. The surprise emerges when we're left expecting more, but cannot figure out when it is going to happen. When these two feelings are sustained, a person can almost feel pain, and even when the cause has dissipated, this sensation can remain for some time after. Burke concludes that these qualities constitute sublime experience.

The literary cave is a sublime space because though it is untouched, preserved and serene, it also contains unknown horrors lurking in its darkness. Shrouded in a veil of mystery, the cave is a location both connoting the beginning of civilization, as well as its end. Its presence in both the history of man and in religious mythology specifically designates it as a mediating site—fertile ground for man's confrontations with life and death, progress and regress, reality and illusion. The figurative cave is embodied by the tensions existing between its conflicting roles as a womb-like shelter safe from the elements, and as the destructive catalyst of ego-death. It was arguably this very tension that enabled 19th century artists and thinkers to utilize the sublime in both Romantic and Gothic works.

The 19th century marked the beginning of an era defined by national anxieties, one of which was the struggle to come to terms with high mortality rates. American life quickly became defined by national mourning.[3] In response to this cultural phenomenon, authors of Gothic literature began to prevalently use the ghost as an allegory for haunting memories of the past, and the spiritual uncertainty of the future. With this supernatural figuration of our cultural pathology, the American people could indirectly confront and come to terms with their trauma at a comfortable distance from reality. Indeed, the Gothic cave is an extension of what Jacques Derrida calls 'hauntology.' When the cave appears in narratives, it is a space where the living go to die, and where the dead come back to life.

In contrast to the Gothic cave, creatives in the 19th century were utilizing qualities of the Romantic genre to create an altogether different kind of space. It is important to contrast these two caves because they contribute to the modern allegorical conception of the cave. In Freudian terms, the Gothic cave represents thanatos, and the Romantic cave represents eros.

In the Romantic cave, our cultural history is preserved, and we are sheltered from the great mysteries of the wild. To get to the core meaning of the Romantic sublime cave, it is worth looking at the work of 19th century American artist Thomas Cole of the Hudson River School of painters. Members of the Hudson River School are revered for their participation in popularizing contemporary American realist painting. They successfully

[3] The rural cemetery movement in the mid-19th-century, for example, sought to relocate graveyards from town centers to larger, more widespread cemeteries on the peripheries of towns—this collectivized the mourning process and united Americans.

captured a feeling previously unutterable to their fellow man: sublimity. Works of the Romantic sublime often utilized skewed perspectives to add a quality of immensity to these natural expanses—unviolated by technological progress. Of the artists in this community, Thomas Cole particularly favored the cave as a symbolic vehicle for transmitting feelings of sublimity, featuring it most notably in *The Voyage of Life* and *Kaaterskill Falls*. He used the artistic medium to visually express and communicate to others his passionate belief in nature as the work of God himself, which he expressed through grandiose displays of heavenly light showering into his landscapes.

At the end of the 19th century and beginning of the Second Industrial Revolution, the magic of electricity and the innovations to follow enabled cave explorations to be performed at previously unexplored depths. Because technologies were progressively decentralizing our place in society through the planned obsolescence of human labor, the concept of the sublime had to be revised

to reflect this new world order. As a result, the paradigmatic roles of light and darkness within the cave were inverted, and our fears became displaced. As the mining industry expanded and the subterranean space became electrified, the language of the sublime was re-appropriated to address technology instead of nature. The new natural landscape was the industrial landscape, and our collective vision of the natural grew increasingly simulated.

In contrast to the Gothic or Romantic sublime, the modern cave is illuminated and becomes what Burke terms artificially infinite: the process by which electricity inverts our conception of the cave as a navigable site of fear and darkness into a traversable, illuminated landscape ripe for discovery. In the artificial infinite cave, the allegories of Plato and Bacon are revised so that action and contemplation need not act as polarized forces. Like the Platonian philosopher emerging from the cave into the painful sunlight, so too must the Baconian subterranean explorer experience pain when his eyes attempt to adjust to the inconceivable darkness. He must succumb ever so slightly to the inevitable madness resultant from his immersion in a pitch black environment and from the destabilizing truths of his archaeological discoveries. However, in this vision of the sublime, the Baconian explorer who endures pain can only create cohesion between his active descent and his lofty contemplations if aided by electricity, or, artificial illumination.

As these dark and mysterious spaces were suddenly transformed into environments amenable to human interaction, the curious went deeper and deeper, discovering a realm far older and more mysterious than what was envisioned by Francis Bacon. Though archaeologists were utilizing genealogical studies to construct a rational past, what was uncovered often had the opposite effect of destabilizing core tenets of our collective social identity. This transition was so drastic, we can even see lasting semantic evidence of our trauma in response to the technological and social upheaval of this era. When we say things like "shed light on," "illuminate us," "in the dark," or "going

Photographs by Charlie Hawks

dark," we are directly referencing the second post-revolution era wherein knowledge, or a connection to the social or technological grid, was defined by allegorical light and darkness.

What the Romantic and Gothic sublime was to early 19th century Americans, the artificial infinite was to late 19th and early 20th century Americans. Though these concepts are tied to different landscapes of meaning and aesthetics, they both create the same response in the human mind: a sustained confusion between states of action and contemplation, expectation and surprise.

The artificially infinite cave, like the Romantic or Gothic cave, functions as a mediator between unceasing technological progress, and the trauma from this progress. What most immediately separates these two caves from one another, however, is that the buried trauma which was figurative in the Romantic and Gothic traditions becomes literal in the artificial sublime. The buried traumas in this new cave are the preserved relics of lost time that threaten to dismantle our imagined pasts. The discovery of the neanderthal skull, for example, was catastrophic to the religious mythology created to prove the primacy of man on Earth. Hence, the cave takes on new roles: both as a space that can shield us from what we don't want to see, and as a vault that can preserve our memories for future generations to uncover. What is fundamental about the transition from the Romantic/Gothic cave to the artificially infinite cave, therefore is the transition from the figurative to the literal, from horror and beauty to science and art.

A genealogy of the (cheese) cave sheds some light on why there is a tendency to improperly ascribe this semantic value to the cheese ripening room. Part of the answer has something to do with the semantic gap discussed earlier, when grotto was improperly defined when adopted into the English language. This might be the only reason, but considering many of the early fermentationists in the United States were Europeans, it is unlikely this is the sole cause. Another answer is simply that fermentation can be kind of disgusting and if we don't have to see it happening (e.g. childbirth, politics, sausage-making), then we can ignore the fact that it ever did. Or, perhaps we treasure ferments so passionately because they offer us the opportunity to assert control over our confrontations with death—something that could arguably be deeply soothing to us.

There are surely many more reasons that can be traced with more time and care. We use cultures to ferment cheese in caves, and we use popular culture to understand the cave. We can return to a ferment to understand more about a culture, and we must descend into the cave to dig up secrets about our cultural past. In this line of thought, maybe we keep cheese in the allegorical cave because it is a little piece of nature's magic that we can never truly understand, and perhaps don't want to. In many ways, fermentation is an almost religious science, and to study it is to attempt to understand the immaterial world—to flood it with light would be to destroy its mystery and autonomy.

WINDOWS

Nicolas

Baird

WE OFTEN USE CAMERAS AS PROXIES FOR OUR EYES, CAPTURING AND RECORDING IMAGES IN A SIMILAR WAY TO HOW OUR EYES PERCEIVE THE WORLD.

But what happens when the camera processes light in a way our eyes can't? While our cameras and our eyes function similarly in many situations, the similarities between these tools break down in extremes. The photographs in this series are un-doctored views of overcast skies taken through cracks and openings in natural rock formations, but because the camera's digital processor is unable to capture extremes of light and dark simultaneously, the landscape is stripped of scale, color, and perspective. Geologic formations photographed in Iceland become indistinguishable from those in southern China, and no identifiable details remain. When we push our tools to their functional limits, the familiar becomes strange: rocks turn into maps, clouds become islands.

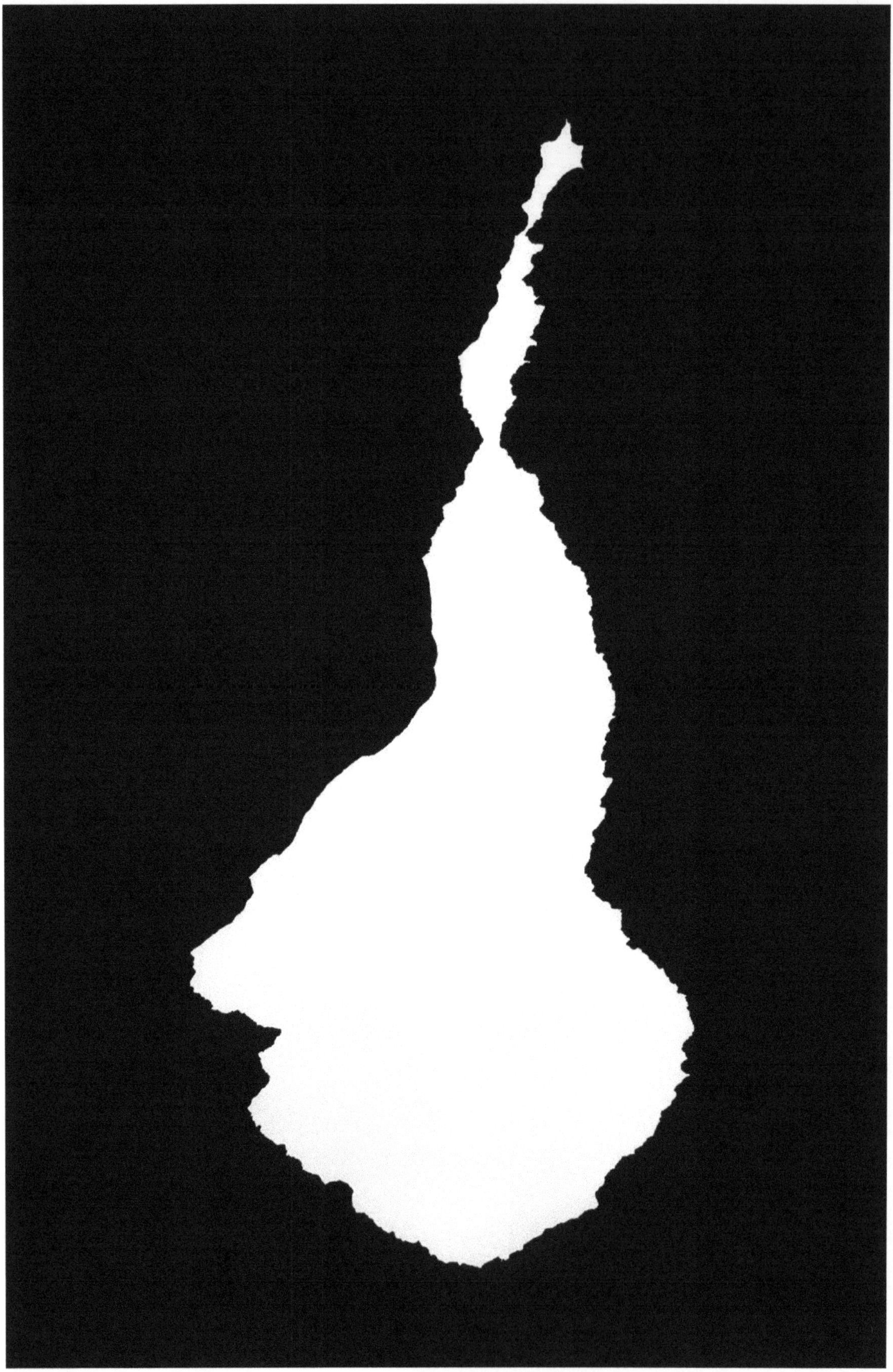

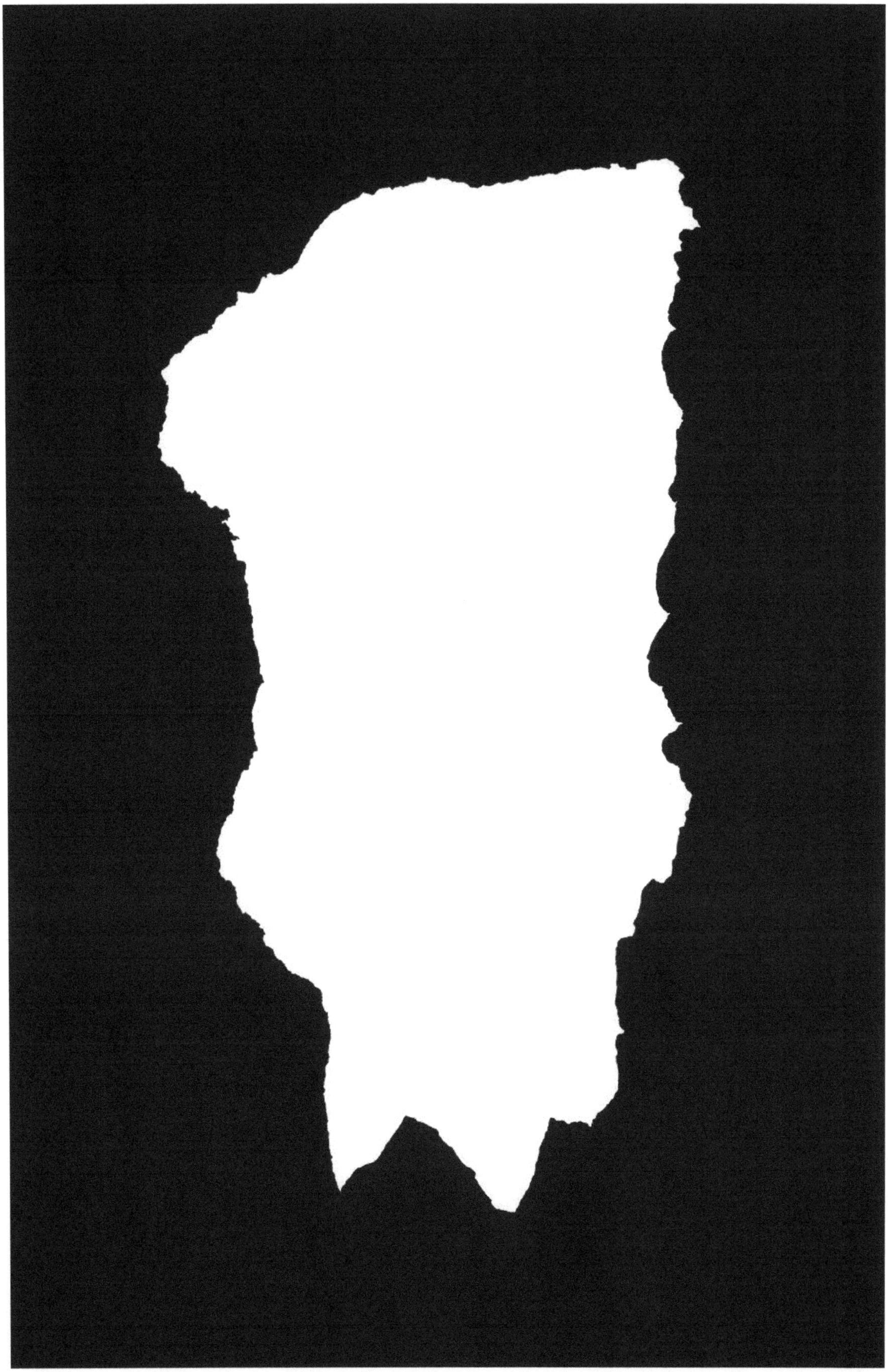

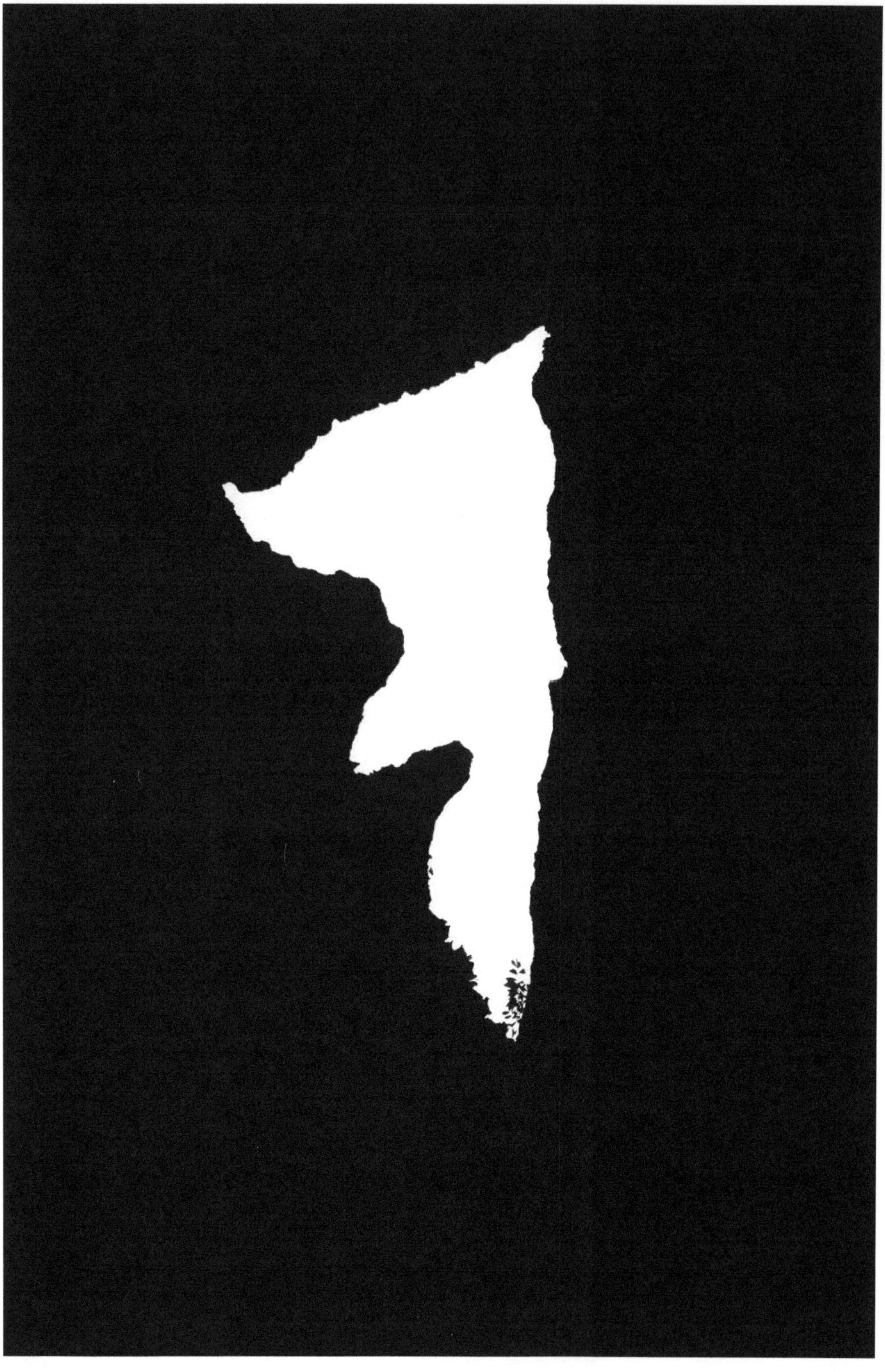

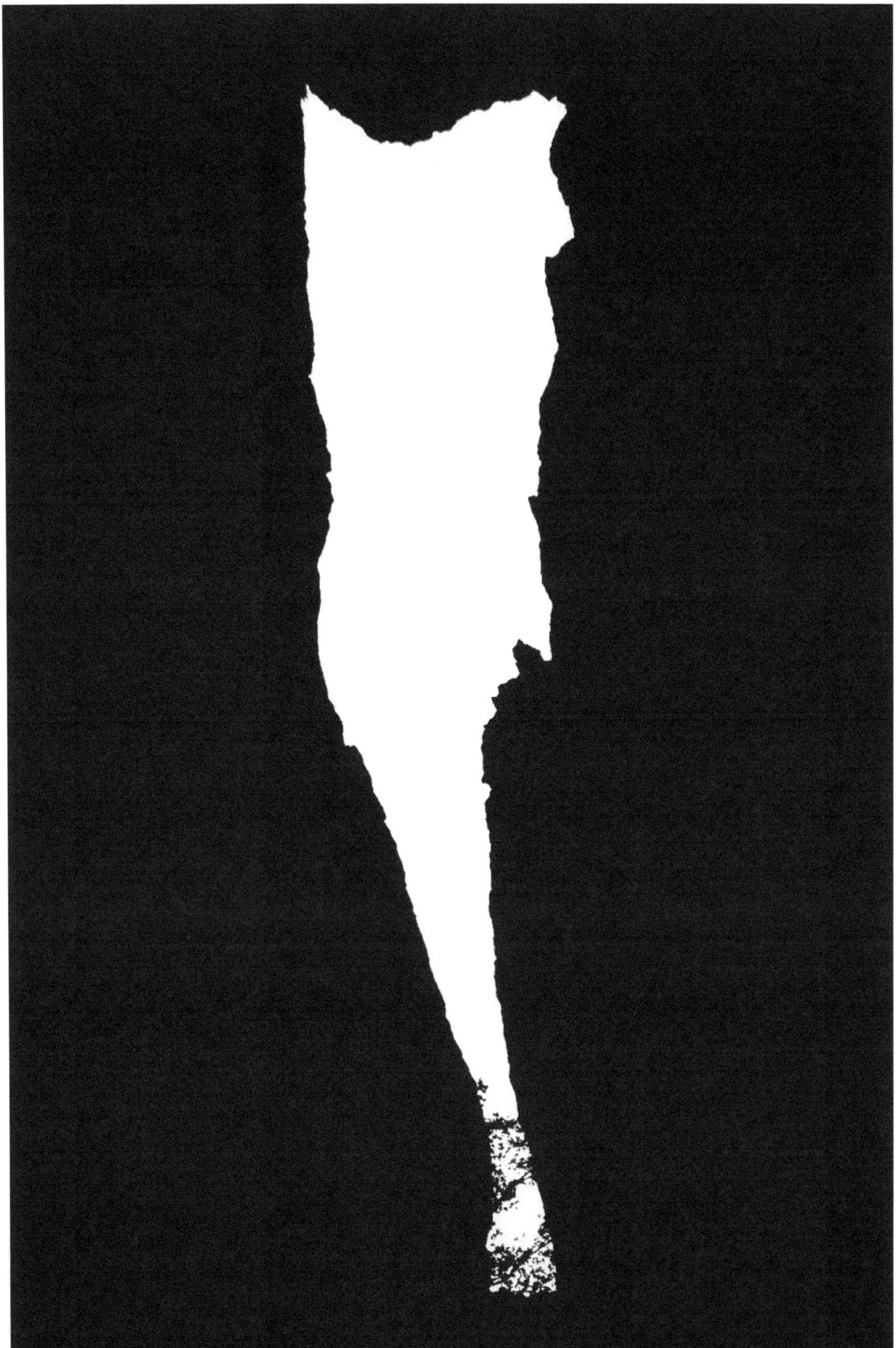

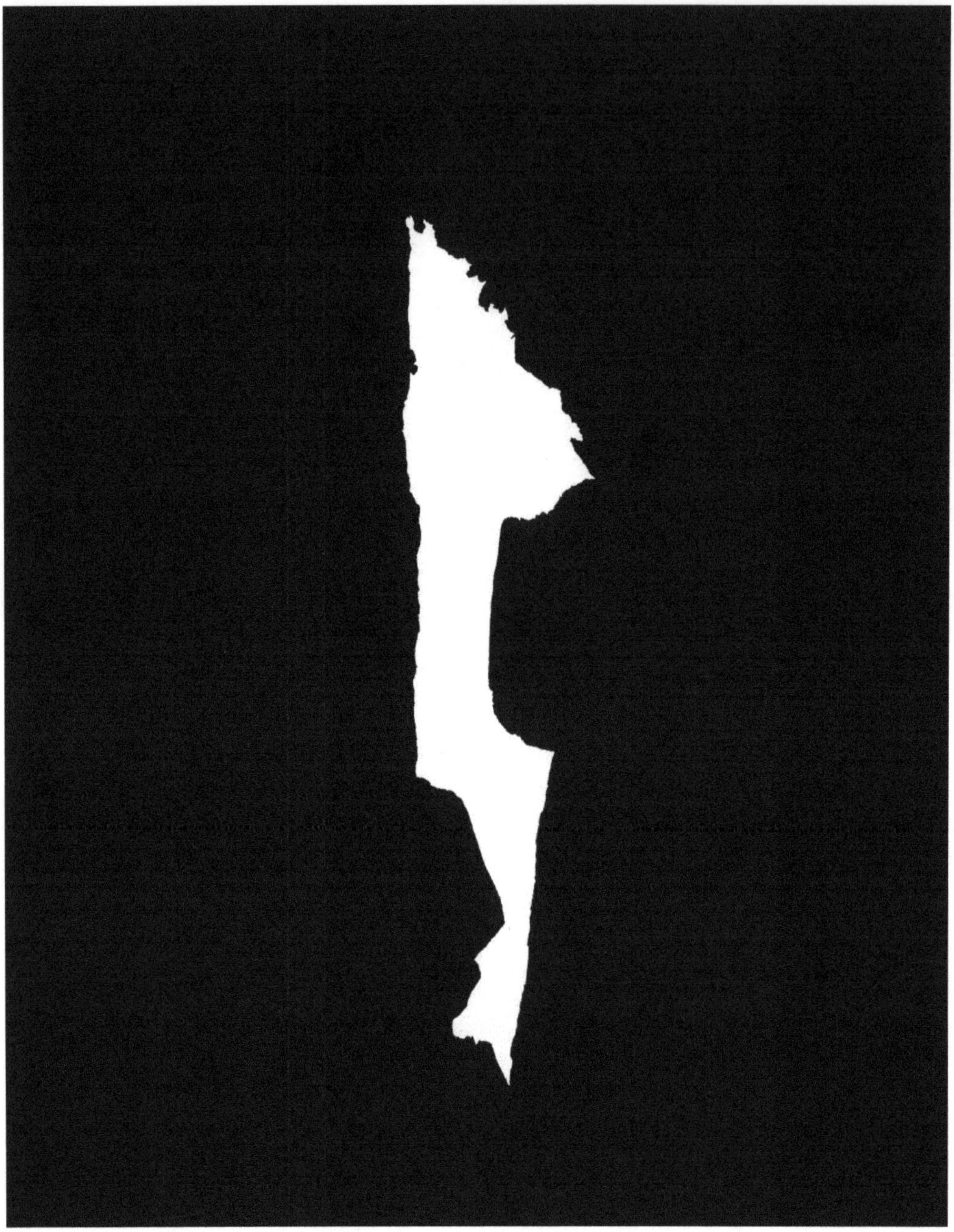

NICOLAS BAIRD

Nicolas Baird is an artist, dancer, and biologist who grew up in Arizona in an adobe house that was a little bit like a cave (very dark in the summer, for staying cool). He currently lives in London where he enjoys pastries, pasties, bubblegum pop, and 70s arthouse films.

 Photograph by Jacquelin Li

MINING ANCIENT KNOWLEDGE FOR MODERN MEDICINE

Sam Anderson

Tarik S., a Lebanese martial arts instructor, can be found most days sitting outside a coffee shop beside a busy Beirut intersection, doling out advice to distraught young people who seek him out. One afternoon I met him there before our training session and found him in pain, wincing and prodding at his swollen chest, "I ate a bit of moomiyo last night," he explained. "It's bat shit. Or something. But it sits in a cave for hundreds of years, so it isn't shit anymore... It gives me too much energy! I did eight hundred push-ups last night, now I can't move!"

Shilajit, or moomiyo as the Russians call it, was claimed to be a cure-all from its earliest mention in a sixth century BCE Sanskrit medical text. This mysterious exudate is found in many of the world's mountain ranges and is thought to be formed by the gradual decomposition of plant and animal matter trapped between layers of rock. When the summer sun warms the mountain, shilajit oozes out from cracks in the stone. Tarik was introduced to shilajit when he lived in Russia, training in the Russian military martial art Systema. He brought back a few jars of the wonder drug prized by the Spetznaz when he returned to Lebanon and consumed it on occasion to enhance his workouts.

MY INTENTION IS NOT TO SUGGEST YOU TRY IT—THAT WOULD BE ILLEGAL AND UNETHICAL, AND MANY COMMERCIAL SHILAJIT BRANDS HAVE BEEN FOUND TO CONTAIN HEAVY METALS LIKE LEAD AND MERCURY.

My own experience taking it was underwhelming, but twenty-six hundred years of tradition prize it as medicine. While shilajit has been studied abroad, traditional medicinal substances are considered "alternative medicine" in the U.S., and American research labs are hesitant to study them. However, a recent study on shilajit from the Laboratory of Cellular and Molecular Neurosciences at the University of Chile ended their paper urging scientists to "break the cultural paradigm" that dismissed potentially valuable substances as alternative medicine and refused to submit them to rigorous molecular and cellular research. This same study suggested that medication for Alzheimer's disease could be derived from shilajit.[1]

The debate is polarizing: advocates of traditional medicine systems laud whatever is the vogue substance as a panacea, and lob the word "profiteer" at pharmaceutical researchers. On the other side is the scientist, who by definition must be a skeptic.

Many of the international studies lack scientific rigor, are conducted only in vitro and not in vivo, or are based on a too small sample size—all valid reasons for American researchers to be skeptical. However, we find ourselves in a double bind in which scientists scorn research of traditional medicines because past research has been imperfect and cursory, while at the same time putting scientists willing to research traditional medicines in the worrying position of being labeled quacks.

This cultural paradigm has been seen with regard to turmeric, food that has become a point of contention between the public and the scientific community. Many of us have heard that turmeric is a potent anti-inflammatory and that curcumin is the medicinal ingredient in turmeric. Some of us have added it to our diet, needing no confirmation beyond the five thousand years it was used as a spice and medicine in the South Asian subcontinent. Yet a quick Internet search reveals legions of US-based scientists quick to scorn turmeric's potential as a medicinal substance.

One such is Ana Gorelova, a specialist in molecular pharmacology from the University of Pittsburgh. In August of 2017, she wrote a harsh condemnation of the pro-turmeric trend, citing a study by the University of Minnesota that found curcumin ineffective as a therapeutic compound. She discouraged further research of turmeric and concluded her article with the declaration that we had all been duped.[2]

Luckily, cancer researchers have been given a bit of leeway to experiment, and the study of turmeric continued. A few months after Gorelova's article, the University of Texas MD Anderson Cancer Center reported that they had studied curcumin-free turmeric and found anticancer effects, indicating that curcumin is not the only compound responsible for turmeric's bioactivity. The same study found that in vitro experiments were not predictive of "potent in vivo antitumor effects of curcumin free turmeric and turmeric." They recommended further research to determine the mode of action, or what exactly is happening at the cellular level.[3]

We should not condemn skeptical scientists. The issue is that potentially valuable medical compounds, often known about by humans for thousands of years, are conflated with other dubious and sometimes-harmful alternative medicine practices hawked by charlatans and naturopaths. One of the agencies responsible for this conflation is the Office of Alternative Medicine—later renamed the National Center for Complementary and Integrative Health.

In 1991, Senator Tom Harkin used his position as chair of the Senate Appropriations Committee to create the OAM after he became convinced he had cured his allergies by eating bee pollen. The first director appointed to the OAM insisted that all research be conducted with rigorous scientific methodology; Senator Harkin did not approve. He pressured the director to resign, drawing the ire of the scientific community. From then on, any research conducted by the OAM was labeled as quackery—and with good reason. However, pseudoscience can only be undone by science. Too many scientists in the U.S. have become dogmatic, scorning potentially life-saving compounds as "alternative medicine."

We may have emerged from the cave of ignorance, but let us not be too quick to dismiss the sum of knowledge that came before we extracted morphine from the poppy. Look at the winding path by which aspirin found its way into our medicine cabinets. The pain and fever-reducing effects of the willow tree were first described in Sumerian clay tablets and the Egyptian Ebbers Papyrus, dating to 1550 BCE. But it wasn't until the mid-eighteenth century that a cleric named Edward Stone experimented with it on a whim. After chewing a bit of willow while suffering from malaria and finding it relieved his symptoms, he gave powdered willow bark to fifty patients with ague The powder alleviated their suffering, and he sent his findings to the Royal Society, who published his letter and ushered willow into the world of accepted science. Eventually, salicylic acid was identified as the active compound, and after well over a hundred years of experimentation, Bayer patented acetylsalicylic acid and began to manufacture Aspirin in bulk.[4] Edward Stone conducted his experiment in this liminal period when natural sciences were still evolving, and medicine was becoming scientific. If the attitudes then had been the same as they are now, Edward Stone might have been dismissed as a quack, and we might not have aspirin in our medicine cabinets today.

---

[1] Carrasco-Gallardo, Carlos, et al. "Shilajit: A Natural Phytocomplex with Potential Procognitive Activity." *International Journal of Alzheimer's Disease*, vol. 2012, 2012, pp. 1–4., doi:10.1155/2012/674142.

[2] Gorelova, Ana. "How Turmeric Became a Naturopathic Cure-All without the Evidence to Back It Up." *Massive*, 3 Aug. 2017, massivesci.com/articles/turmeric-wellness-supplement-bad-science.

[3] Prasad, Sahdeo, et al. "Curcumin-Free Turmeric Exhibits Activity against Human HCT-116 Colon Tumor Xenograft: Comparison with Curcumin and Whole Turmeric." *Frontiers in Pharmacology*, vol. 8, Dec. 2017, doi:10.3389/fphar.2017.00871.

[4] *Clinical Pharmacist*, September 2014, Vol 6, No 7, online | DOI: 10.1211/CP.2014.20066661

WHAT TO DO WHEN TRAPPED IN A CAVE

ANSWERS WILL BE AVAILABLE ON OUR BLOG AT DISHRAGMAG.COM/BLOG

ACROSS

1 "Back in Black" band
5 Marseille entry in 1 across' genre
9 "___! What fray was here?": Romeo
12 "You've got ___!"
13 Irish farewell
14 Checker, perhaps
16 ___ Nova
17 Distress signal
18 Parasitic arachnid
19 Porsche mod.
20 Seven, old style
22 Volcanic type buried Pompeii
24 Word used to connote a maiden name
25 Convert, with "over"
26 Carols
28 Russian peninsula
31 Mozart's "L'___ del Cairo"
34 Frequency measure (Abbr.)
35 Expressed surprise
36 Pitcher ___ Hershiser
38 Observe
42 Not a frequent typo
43 Former Portuguese province on the south coast of China
44 Code-cracking org.
45 Van man who lost his ear
47 File type a 3D animator might use
48 Dead center?
49 Like collegiate dicts.
51 Undertake, with "out"
53 Kind of market
54 Habsburg alphabetic device
57 Kind of dance mus.
59 Prefix meaning united
60 Accounting major's deg.
63 Be seeing you, on the web
64 Big bell in London
67 Heavy, durable furniture wood
69 Machu Picchu builder
71 Actor ___ Hirsch
73 Actress ___ Lenska
74 "Back to the Future" antagonist
75 Spokes
76 Polite email wd.
77 Man or Wight, e.g.
78 "Frozen" reindeer

DOWN

1 "I wouldn't send --- out in this."
2 ___ la vie
3 "___ Boot" (1981 war film)
4 Corns
5 "La Bamba" actor --- Morales
6 Fond treatment (Abbr.)
7 Laugh
8 Super Mario World console: Abbr.
9 Beyond reasonable limits
10 Where you might find some great blueberry pie
11 Shine
12 Simplicity simile
15 Mike's candy is also ____
21 Queen of Thebes
23 Hydrogen isocyanide formula
25 Large amount of money
27 ___Kosh B'gosh
28 King ape
29 "___ Be In Love," Kate Bush song
30 Carroll of "Spellbound"
32 Black diamond
33 Bows for strings
34 The Dutch Royal Air Force
37 "___ on Down the Road"
39 Chem. finisher
40 Salinger dedicatee
41 Yaba ___ doo
43 The least you can eat (Abbr.)
46 Vietnamese coin
48 An acronym for radical supporters of el president naranja
50 Address to a fella
52 Examine a case
54 Carl Sagan's subj.
55 Ogle
56 As a whole
58 Mets and Marlins, e.g. (Abbr.)
61 Israel's Netanyahu, familiarly
62 French cordial flavoring
63 ___ noir
64 Tarry
65 Tiger Woods's ex
66 "In the," in Italy
68 Egyptian spirits
70 What might be on TV if the Eskimos, Argonauts or Blue Bombers are playing
72 Dallas basketball player, for short

Illustrations by Cassie Tucker

I LIVE IN A CAVE!
CAVE CASE
Brian Blomerth
I LOVE MY CAVE!
TO ACQUIRE A CAVE LIKE THIS... FIRST LOCATE THE CAVE HERMIT!
THEN KICK HIM OUT!
WHACK!

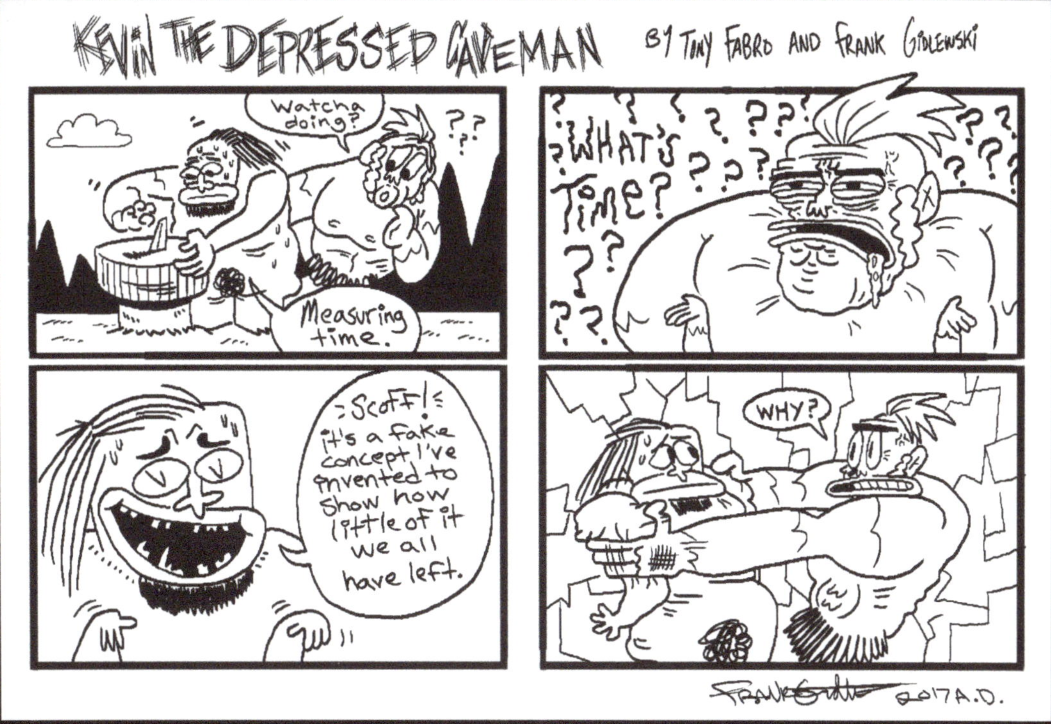
KEVIN THE DEPRESSED CAVEMAN
BY TONY FABRO AND FRANK GIDLEWSKI
Watcha doing?
Measuring time.
WHAT'S TIME?
SCOFF!
it's a fake concept I've invented to show how little of it we all have left.
WHY?
2017 A.D.

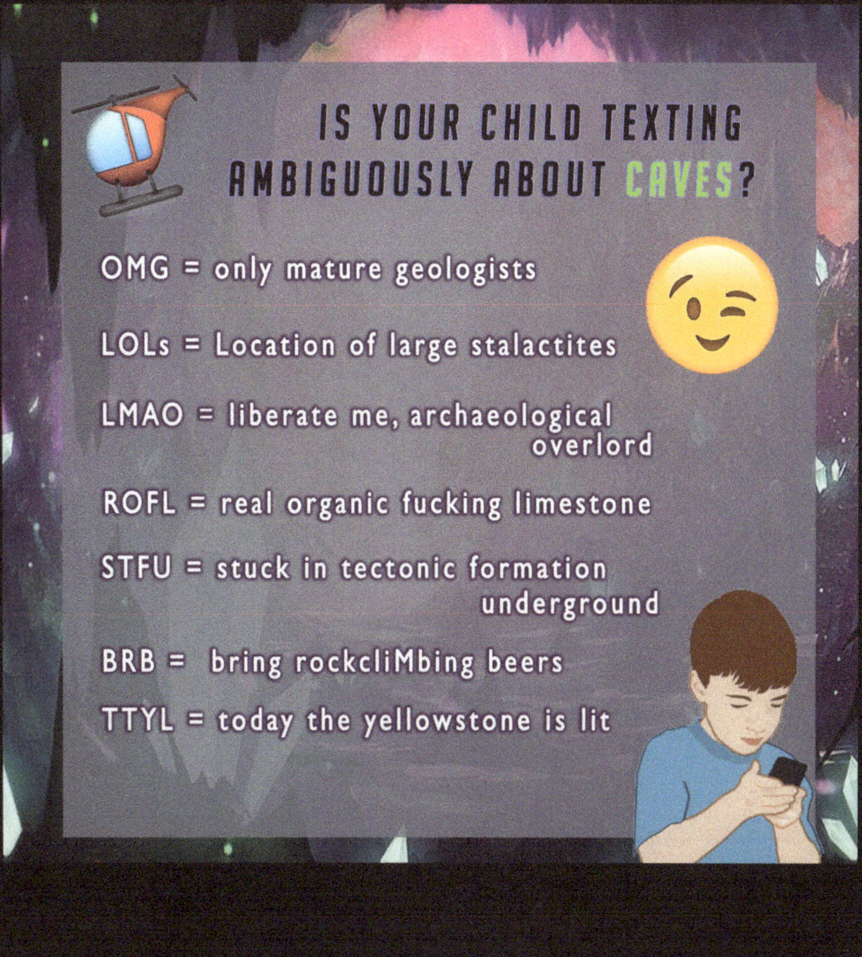
IS YOUR CHILD TEXTING AMBIGUOUSLY ABOUT CAVES?
OMG = only mature geologists
LOLs = Location of large stalactites
LMAO = liberate me, archaeological overlord
ROFL = real organic fucking limestone
STFU = stuck in tectonic formation underground
BRB = bring rockcliMbing beers
TTYL = today the yellowstone is lit

CPSIA information can be obtained
at www.ICGtesting.com
Printed in the USA
BVHW02s0352010918
526197BV00005B/6/P

9 781643 161075